Comments about
Fingers Pointing Toward the Sacre

"Frederick Frank is that rarest of human beings words, 'catholic, generic.' In touch with the pere metaphors sally from Japanese tea ceremony to Me   to Tibetan devotions. And withall his drawingshis beau   passionate, clear-eyed drawings!"
> Robert Aitken, author of *Taking the Path of Zen*

"A work of art and love [*A Pilgrimage to Now/Here*]. His skill with language, his striking drawings as illustrations, and his extraordinary candor, whether dealing with other people or himself, set this book aside as utterly unique. One simply finds oneself alone with Franck in the thoughtful and exuberant pilgrimage itself."
> Malcolm Boyd, from a review of *Pilgrimage to Now/Here* in *The Christian Century*

"A charming volume [*A Pilgrimage to Now/Here*] . . . you have captured in your pages many delicious flashes of the life and light of the Orient."
> Joseph Campbell, author of *The Power of Myth*

"I . . . was deeply impressed by the way he could combine a subtle but thorough appreciation for Japanese religion and culture without feeling he had to diminish his serious Christian spirituality. A person capable of drawing on a variety of spiritual traditions without becoming superficial. I sometimes beleive his artist's eye must be the secret. He simply *sees* things most people do not, and he does not get lost in conceptual comparisons. Enchanting narrative quality. . . . A rare book."
> Harvey Cox, author of *Many Mansions*

"In word and image this thoughtful work captures a pilgrimage, at once external and internal, which can illumine the path for all seekers of the truth that lies behind the phantasma of everyday existence. Franck . . . looks deep into the human heart and what he finds there is the priceless treasure of the sacred reality: a discovery and a message so crucial to contemporary humanity."
> Georg Feuerstein, author of *Sacred Paths*

"Frederick Franck has given us another book of wisdom. In his quest to find the resonances between Christian spirituality and Buddhism, he acts as a bridge himself. His sincere dialogues with the spiritual masters of the East show us the possibility of a universal ecumenism that is rarely experienced. Franck's wonderful spider line drawings reflect the numinous experience of

his sojourn to the East. *Fingers Pointing Toward the Sacred* is a treasure for those who are on or seek a spiritual journey."
 Matthew Fox, author of *The Reinvention of Work*

"Frederick Franck's new book is his best, the fruit of a long and rich life of bridge-building between East and West. Every page is filled with insight and wisdom that flows from a free and compassionate heart. It deserves a wide and universal audience."
 Brother Patrick Hart, O.C.S.O., Abbey of Gethsemani, Trappist, Kentucky

"The secret of all the great religious traditions is loving attentiveness, and the well-being of the planet will rely more and more on human beings—of whatever tradition—paying attention to one another in playfulness, reverence, and compassion. Frederick Franck is a pioneer in seeking and seeing that which builds human beings spiritually together. This is a gracious book . . . quietly challenging to the reader to see his or her own longing in the light of a tradition other than the known and familiar."
 Alan Jones, Dean of Grace Cathedral, San Francisco, California

"For the pilgrim in each of us who would journey into Eastern and Western spiritual traditions to chart a path in this troubled time, what better companion than Frederick Franck? His wise, witty, compassionate observations—in lively words and livelier drawings—jolt us awake to the wealth of our planetary heritage."
 Joanna Macy, author of *World as Lover, World as Self*

"Frederick Franck here attempts through words to go beyond words, through drawings to reach the inner eye. His fingers point relentlessly toward the "human face divine" (Milton) and those who are able to see will take off their shoes. An illuminating companion for the barefoot pilgrimage."
 Virginia Mollenkott, author of *Sensous Spirituality: Out from Fundamentalism*

"The beauty of this book lies not only in its theme—the eternal search for the heart of religion—and not only in its acknowledgment that the well meditated question is more important than any given answer, but also in the way Frederick Franck reconciles the archetypal journey with his personal history and with the modern world. Most important, he tells a good story, he tells it well, and the story he tells is an ancient one revisited—exactly what we wonderers and wanderers need."
 Thomas Moore, author of *Care of the Soul* and *Soul Mates*

"A journey by one man that becomes a hymn to all that is truly human. Franck blends his artistic gifts, infectious wit, and powers of observation to create a book that informs the mind and forms the heart longing, as he does, for encounter with the Sacred. Where Franck's fingers point, we twentieth-century pilgrims committed to world peace would do well to follow."
 Susan Muto, author of *Pathways of Spiritual Living*

"Frederick Franck is one of a rare and precious breed—an authentic troubadour whose lyricism is pure in word and image. He quietly roams our materialistic world and shows us that even here, even now, there is hope for our soul."
Jacob Needleman, author of *Money and the Meaning of Life*

"In our times of devastating tourism, even spiritual tourism, it is exhilarating and comforting to read the vivid recollections of an artist and a thinker who succeeds in clothing in simple language the most burning issues of our times in conversations with remarkable personalities of Asia. You will learn as much, if not more, about spirituality and comparative religion from his narrative than from more abstract and apparently profound books. Sometimes you feel that his finger does not only point toward the Sacred, but that he touches it."
Raimon Panikkar, author of *Silence of God*

"The best introduction to macro-ecumenism getting religions together to work under their deep commonalities. Frederick uses his personal journey towards the universal sacred, to make the case for the only viable, panentheist attitude to that universal reality."
Rustum Roy, professor at Pennsylvania State University

"For Frederick Franck it is of the utmost importance to find in the diversities of the philosophies and the religions, in the diversity of the people he encounters, the common bond between all of humanity . . . his words and drawings make us see the world as a place where, with more understanding and tolerance, we could all live together in harmony."
Rhena Schweitzer Miller, daughter of Albert Schweitzer

"The encounter between Christianity and the religions of the East is one of the most significant spiritual phenomena of the late twentieth century. Frederick Franck invites us to explore with him some of the promises and pitfalls of this encounter. His focus on the mystical and experiential dimensions of these spiritual pathways offers a welcome relief to the squabbles over dogma taking place in many ecumenical dialogues between these traditions. It is only by listening to each other as we describe our experiences that we begin to learn what we have in common and how we differ. Frederick Franck has helped us all to be better listeners."
Philip St. Romain, author of *Kundalini Energy and Christian Spirituality*

"Frederick Frank has gone beyond all formal religion and any one tradition in order to plung into the inner streams of mystrical wisdom found in all of the great world religions. He has discovered the eternal reality of Spirituality at the heart of the religions. His descriptions, assimilations of insights and reflections are gems. His is a plea for a spirituility come of age, one that is open to all traditions."
Brother Wayne Teasdale. member of Monastic Interreligious Dialogue

FINGERS POINTING
TOWARD THE SACRED

Also by Frederick Franck

Open Wide, Please!	1955
Days with Albert Schweitzer	1959
My Friend in Africa	1960
African Sketchbook	1961
My Eye Is in Love	1963
Outsider in the Vatican	1965
I Love Life	1967
Exploding Church	1968
Simenon's Paris	1970
The Zen of Seeing	1973
Pilgrimage to Now/Here	1973
An Encounter with Oomoto	1975
The Book of Angelus Silesius	1976
Zen and Zen Classics, Selections From R. H. Blyth, ed.	1977
Every One, The Timeless Myth of Everyman Reborn	1978
The Awakened Eye	1979
Art As a Way	1981
The Supreme Koan	1982
The Buddha Eye: An Anthology fo the Kyoto School, ed.	1982
Echoes from the Bottomless Well	1985
Life Drawing Life	1989
A Little Compendium on That Which Matters	1989
Zen Seeing, Zen Drawing: Meditation in Action	1993
Drawings of Lambaréné: Albert Schweitzer's Hospital in Action	1994

Readers:

Au Pays du Soleil	1958
Au Fil de l'Eau	1964
Croquis Parisiens	1969
Tutte le Strade Portano a Roma	1970

Pt. 1 of this book

Some of Pt. 2 of this book

FINGERS POINTING TOWARD THE SACRED

*A Twentieth Century Pilgrimage on the
Eastern and Western Way*

Frederick Franck

with drawings by the author

**BEACON POINT
P R E S S**

BEACON POINT PRESS
Junction City, Oregon

BEACON POINT
P R E S S

Beacon Point Press
P.O. Box 460
Junction City, OR 97448

Pilgrimage to Now/Here was orignially published by Orbis Books.
A portion of *Road Signs Along the Way* was published as *The Supreme
Koan* by the Crossroad Publishing Company.

Book design by Ruth Cottrell Books
Typography by Conch Composition

Cover design by Steve Naegele Design

Printed by NcNaughton & Gunn, Inc.

ISBN 1-56907-006-7
Library of Congress Catalog Card Number 94-71670

Printed in the United States of America

1 2 3 4 5 6 – 99 98 97 96 95 94

For Claske
and for Lukas

When the Emperor of China asked the great Bodhidharma to explain the Sacred, the sage shrugged, "Nothing Sacred, just a vast openness." Could that perhaps imply that all is sacred, these mountains, rivers, the whole great earth with all that lives on it?

✥ *Acknowledgments* ✥

By way of acknowledgments I quote some sayings that come to mind very often. To their authors I owe infinite gratitude.

The meaning of life is to see. *Hui Neng*

Zen and Christianity are the future. *Thomas Merton*

As far as the Buddha Nature is concerned, there is no difference between sinner and sage. . . . One enlightened thought and one is a Buddha, one foolish thought and one is a common man. *Hui Neng*

In every soul, even that of the greatest sinner, God dwells and is substantially present. *Saint John of the Cross*

Become angry and you turn the Unborn, the Buddha Mind, into a Fighting Demon, vent your selfishness and change it into a Hungry Ghost, give rise to your folly and make it into an animal. *Bankei*

God is a common light and a common splendor, illuminating everything in heaven and earth according to its need and worth. *Jan van Ruysbroeck*

If you seek the Buddha outside of yourself, the Buddha turns into a devil. *Dōgen*

If you use It, It will make you live. If you don't, It will destroy you. *The Gospel according to Thomas*

Your treasure house is within you. It contains all you need. *Hui Hai*

God is my Ground, I am God's Ground. *Meister Eckhart*

"What is the Buddha?" *Joshu* answered: "The oak tree in the front yard."

I ask to be rid of God, that is, that God by His Grace would bring me into the essence that is above God and above all distinctions. *Meister Eckhart*

Nothingness Thou art
fathomless Abyss.
To see Abyss in all that is
is seeing that which is. *Angelus Silesius*

When the wheel turns
Sunyata gnashes its teeth. *Daito*

Johan Sebastian Bach: All his preludes, fuges, contatas—every page!

Contents

Acknowledgments   xi

Prologue

A Prologue Not to Be Skipped   3

Part One - Pilgrimage to Now/Here

Flight   7
Sri Lanka   21
Madras   47
Dharamsala   69
Hong Kong-Toyko   107
Kyoto   119
Nō Drama   153
Stirrings of the Spirit   167

Part Two - Road Signs Along the Way

Putting Oneself on the Line   193
Unfathomable Grace, Immeasurable Curse   201
Zen: The Homeground Rediscovered   217
A Heart Full of Awe   223
The Specifically Human Confirmed by Modern
   Science   229
What Remained on the Filter   233
Fingers Pointing   243
A Sequence of Incarnations   247
A Love Affair Rekindled   249
Nihilism Unmasked   263
Fellow Wayfarers   269
Coda   275
The Unkillable Human   279

Glossary   281
About the Author   285

❧ *Prologue* ❧

⚘ A Prologue Not to Be Skipped ⚘

This book consists of two parts. Part One is a relived travelogue, a "spiritual" travelogue I might say, through Sri Lanka, India, the Himalayas, and Japan, some years ago.

Part Two continues this pilgrimage— this search for Meaning that goes on until one's last day—against the less exotic backdrop of Warwick, New York, and a place called Pacem in Terris I built there.

Soon it will become all too clear that the one who writes this is neither philosopher nor theologian nor scholar, but simply an artist, one of those right-brainers whose left hemisphere—due to the limited capacity of the human skull—may be somewhat undersized. Right-brainers have the reputation of being harebrainers in certain quarters, which may explain why I dare start this not unserious record of a long pilgrimage by relating a dream:

> I am relaxing in my deck chair. We are gliding on a becalmed endless expanse of pale blue northern Atlantic. I watch another iceberg approaching, sure it will slide past like the previous one. If not, we'll give it a gentle little push!
>
> My fellow passengers are playing deck tennis or strolling, squinting through their binoculars at the blinding light reflected on glistening sugar loaves of ice. Smiling stewards offer Delft blue cups of mid-moring broth steaming in the cold air. Women in mink and nutria lean against the railing watching the men in cashmere sweaters playing deck tennis.
>
> The sugar loaf, this time, does not float past. An almost inaudible scraping of the hull . . . a slight shiver runs through the ship's spine. The strollers stop wideeyed, stand as if frozen. The ship starts to list almost imperceptibly. Do I hear the band intone, "Nearer My God to Thee"?

Silence. The sea lies motionless. No more trace of the great Ship of Fools . . . and I woke up.

One of the most convincing proofs of the goodness of life may be that even after the worst nightmares you wake up.

Still, this one, more than a nightmare, must have been a wakeup call. For we are obviously all in the same boat on our collision course with the unyielding iceberg of Reality. It might be high time to change course from the technologization, our computerization of human life, and to switch from the conceit of our immense know-how to questioning once again the Why.

It was for no other reason than my preoccupation with this Why—a "spiritual" one, I admit—that some years ago I boarded a plane to set out on the Oriental intermezzo of my life's pilgrimage, that forms Part One of this book.

Part One

✤ *Pilgrimage to Now/Here* ✤

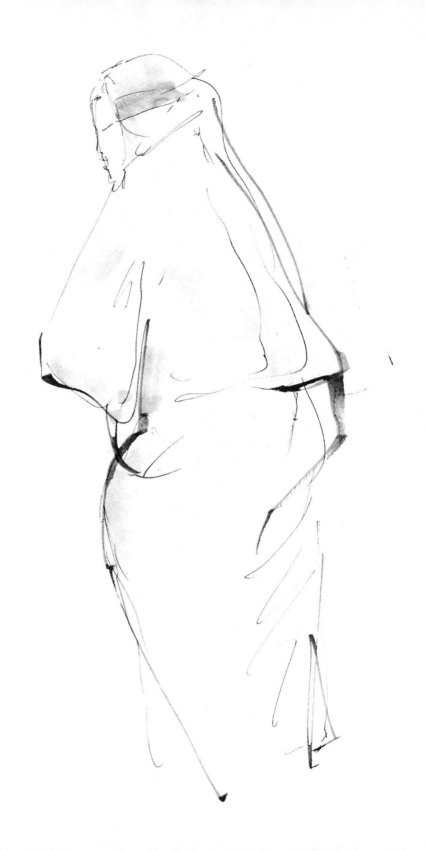

⚓ *Flight* ⚓

I am all too surrounded by thin air. Too deep below, by way of terra firma, lies endless desert. Separated from the infinity of space by a thin skin of aluminum, I am propelled at 600 mph by four infernal engines. Who of my fellow passengers will get up and, calmly covering us with a lethal weapon, move to the cabin up front? What engine lies ticking in the luggage compartment? What insane fellow traveler will do what, to make this hurtling minimodel of society disappear without a trace?

I used to be terrified while flying, could neither read nor sleep. I was jealous of the man studying the *Wall Street Journal*, the girl glancing at *Vogue*, the woman snoring quietly. Gradually I discovered how flying sharpened my perception. Fear became replaced by awareness that turned into contemplation, into deep quietude. Now I can read, on the edge of infinity. Never novels or magazines, but Chuang-Tzu, Hui Neng, the first chapter of the St. John's gospel. These marvels, too often reread on earth, regain pristine freshness, become crystals of revelation in the stratosphere. My eye wanders through the fuselage. It sees the girl skimming *Vogue*, her standard-beautiful legs crossed. Before my eye she changes from baby to girl to mother to grandmother to corpse. I perceive this metamorphosis, my eye fixed on the tendon that runs laterally from her knee to her thigh. No longer deflected by the automatic, unwhistled wolf-whistle, I see her as she is, encapsulated in the cocoon of a short-eternal life of her own, which happens to be synchronized with mine; both to end abruptly if the thin metallic skin should give way and we'd be flung into space, colliding falling leaves.

Up here all becomes almost palpably *maya*, cosmic illusion, deceptive appearance. Yet not sheer hallucination am I. I am just all too relatively real and, in this relative reality, pain and death are such absolute and real horrors. If the end should come seconds from now and we'd all explode together like gnats against the windshield, the girl's last conscious thought might be "skirt length," my neighbor's "Standard Oil." My own? No better. All three of us would be thinking of trivialities with the surface of our minds. Deep below—or above—that conscious surface-mind, overstuffed with manipulative know-how, far below the level of the Freudian unconscious, their minds and mine, I know, are in eternal, unborn contemplation. So perhaps is the mind of the animal.

But, born human, I have the kind of consciousness designed to be aware of this contemplation within, quintessence of my not being cockroach but man, contemporary man.

Contemporary man. Man without fixed abode. No longer does he live in an environment. He exists in a context, a context that is constantly shifting, nationally, culturally, religiously, ecologically, politically. Here I am, flying in a context, shifting at the speed of sound. A mere specimen of contemporary man am I, that homeless adventurer against his will, that involuntary globetrotter, whose travel agent is the nightmare-idol we call history, who is chased from his home ground by economic disaster, by political or racial persecution, by war and rumors of war, partitions, revolutions. Even if, for the time being, he escapes these involuntary wanderings, he is driven to fly all over the globe as tourist, businessman, executive, researcher, do-gooder.

Compelled to stay put, he instantly becomes a vicarious globetrotter, daily uprooted by radio, television, and newspaper to be immersed in the conflicts, the violence, the horrors, the ideas and ideologies, the fads, the religions, the superstitions, and pseudo-religions of all seven continents. Mobility, no longer purely geographical and social, has become a total mobility into the onrushing future of ever-accelerated change, but that does not change what Matters.

In response to our ever-shifting context, our shifting "Me" seems to form itself, a Me constantly changing, adapting itself by chains of action-reaction to the uncatalogued, unclassifiable, infinite chaos of cultural, technological, political stimuli, influences, and conventions. This Me contains my whole lexicon of notions about world, nature, man, God, Christ, nation, race, self, no-self.

And yet, within and beyond this changing chameleon-like Me, something within is aware of something unassailable, undefiled, an unbounded capacity for experience, a core of stillness in the midst of all agitation, continuously hearing, touching, tasting, smelling, and above all seeing, seeing and perceiving, be it through the distorting, synthetic filter of the overconditioned Me.

Is this "something" I?

The eye, the I, is a mirror. It is the I that sees, that makes my hand move and draw. It is the image in the mirror of this eye that is transmitted through this heart and this entire organism to my hand, its seismograph. Hence the drawing bears the authentic imprint of "my" organism, like a fingerprint, the only "originality" I aspire to. The Me is that which talks, writes, copes, manages, manipulates. When it writes about the I, the Me mumbles from memory. The I, hardly ever glimpsed, is incommunicado, unattainable.

The candle of the body is this eye. This eye is I.

Our context lands with a bump at Istanbul airport, chaotic and dirty as a bus station.

I stand on a balcony of the old Park Hotel. Deep below lies Istanbul, a silent dead crater of blackness. Beyond it the Bosporus, a sheet of moonlight without ripple.

From the terrifying sleep of Istanbul—once Byzantium, once Constantinople—a surf of mute sobs and moans breaks in wave after wave of silent agony against my balcony. Centuries gasp their anguish. Ice-cold I crawl back into the decrepit hotel bed. My fingers feel my flesh as meat, still alive, already dead. I feel my flesh as old, as young, as male, as female. Flesh of my grandfather, my mother, my son. I switch on the light. The faded curtains are the color of rotten strawberries, caked blood.

"Never shall I forget this as long as I live."

Thoughts of the rut! How long will you live! Whence this compulsion to see Naples, since we must die? Why then this

Istanbul

pilgrimage to Sri Lanka, India, Japan, you fool, you jet-Wandering Jew?

The legend says that the Wandering Jew must wander through the world until he acknowledges Christ. Who is this Christ? The idol on the crucifix, used as a pretext for countless tortures, burnings? I get up. See my face in the mirror. Sallow, bloated, old and hateful. What Christ? In my mind an answer echoes: "In all faces I see the Face of faces, veiled as in a riddle." Where did I read this? Nicholas of Cusa? Even in this face in the mirror?

All wandering, every pilgrimage, is a safari that leads through the jungles of our darkest interior. To Now/Here. Then why depart?

It is the interior that calls us, pilgrims, on pilgrimage. The others go on cruises, on trips.

It is all pilgrimage. Mine started in Maastricht, a border town where Holland touches Belgium and Germany, a good place for a pilgrim to be born: trilingually, multiculturally, as a congenital borderline case.

It started in earnest when, as a small boy, I first escaped from my agnostic-humanist family-island-in-a-Catholic-sea—slinking into the Romanesque basilica around the corner to kneel surreptitiously before the sad, bleeding Jesus in a cloud of incense. He rose in glory into the new-blue sky over the river Meuse, a deathless meadowlark.

A child's ecstasy, until face-to-face with his ambassador, the double-chinned pastor with the stinking cigar.

This happened during the First World War. I was five years old when the continuum of horror known as the twentieth century started. In my memory the sky stayed blood red and the guns boomed all through my childhood. I was to remain allergic to violence and war forever.

Since then the Kaiser's, the Austro-Hungarian, and the British empires, the Weimar Republic, the Thousand Year Reich, the

Roman Catholic monolith, and the American Dream have all collapsed like jellies in the sun and as we approach the year 2000, we are in panic that the earth itself will die. It is not unlike the expectation of the end of the world in the year 1000. The end is now far more probable, but the Second Coming does not seem as imminent as last time. Or is it? There are strange signs in the sky. Could the Second Coming be incognito?

Today at noon, Istanbul's muezzins pray from the minarets of five hundred mosques. Loudspeakers bellow the ineffable name—on tape?—high over the heads of crowds that keep pushing themselves into overfilled buses. Coolies bent double under incredible loads keep stumbling their way through the compact human mass. Riverboats and ferries, trucks and jets continue their clanging and roaring. Taxis rush blaring across Ataturk Bridge. Under the bridge the lone figure of an old man kneels down on a prayer mat, bowing rhythmically. His buttocks glow in the vertical sun.

Already Istanbul is fading from view, a picture-postcard taken with a telelens. Down below in the Sea of Mamara float soft-green and ochre islands. White dinky-toy steamers leave long indigo feathers of wake. On each there must be life-size men. One always forgets, being blind.

Weird to watch the film roll back, here at 30,000 feet above a rust-red desert! Was it Me who once studied medicine in Amsterdam, dentistry—of all things—in Edinburgh, was an anesthetist in Pittsburgh? Was it Me who painted landscapes in a London studio, in Brisbane, in Greenwich Village, who built up a practice off Madison Avenue (private practice, that last of the pushcart enterprises, be it with humanitarian pretension), who married and divorced, was it Me?

What is there left of the Me that incised abscesses and sketched at Albert Schweitzer's hospital in Lambaréné, who wrote those books, who had those exhibitions? What has actually survived of that Me? Is my or anyone else's autobiography anything but a stranger's string of anecdotes linked together as a true-life story?

And yet, when on that October day in 1962 I heard John XXIII make his opening speech to the Second Vatican Council he had called, it was like the ringing of the bells on Easter morning and the rising of the meadowlark. "It is only dawn," the old man had exclaimed in the midst of the Cuban missile crisis. He was obviously more than just a pope, this Enlightened One, who happened to be pope. His Council, I felt, was going to be the crucial spiritual event of my lifetime. I flew to Rome to do hundreds of drawings of the drama and its actors during Vatican II's four sessions. I shared the euphoria when Angelo Roncalli threw the windows open, and the despondence when he died and they were being pushed shut once more. Vatican II became indeed a watershed, if not the way anyone, except perhaps the Spirit, had planned it.

The plane shudders, seat-belt warnings go on. The desert has disappeared. On the left billowing cloud-castles, on the right deep charcoal grey with flashes of lightning. I close my eyes. Three days ago I landed once more in Rome. What is a pilgrimage that skips Rome?

Again I stood in the Piazza San Pietro, on the very spot where on that sunny Thursday, December 8, 1962 I had been sketching what the papers used to call "the purple waterfall" of three thousand cardinals and bishops walking, shuffling, limping down the steps of St. Peter's at the end of the daily session to their waiting limousines and buses. That day all lingered in the piazza, for Pope John was going to give his blessing. The window opened, and there, with the cancer inside him gnawing him away, stood Angelo Roncalli smiling and waving, spreading out his arms as if to embrace the whole world. His strong voice came over the loudspeakers, "Slowly, slowly I am coming up. Sickness, then convalescence! What a spectacle before me today! The whole church standing here together!"

Sick Pope John at the window

And then he started to sing. Of course he knew, as we all did, that he was dying. But the vigorous gravelly Italian voice sang as if there were no death.

It seems centuries ago. For a flash Rome, once more, was a capital of hope, was once more *axis mundi*—for the last time? God had once more been on the verge of revealing himself in his aspect of goodness.

Did the voice over the intercom mumble that we are crossing Arabia? One never understands.

When in the edifice guaranteed to contain the perfect, complete truth about all the universe, the windows were thrown open by a pope and the fresh air came rushing in, disturbing centuries of cobwebs. Instead of staying quietly, hardly noticeable, in corners and under cabinets, centuries of torn webs were blown all over the red plush of gilded thrones, turned the exquisite interior into a shambles, so that one was embarrassed to receive visitors.

Once Pope John was safely dead, the desperate housekeepers slaved overtime for years to get the cobwebs pushed back under the cabinets and into the corners where they belong, until, at last the palace was beginning to look respectable again.

From its powerful radio transmitters the Vatican still broadcasts the tidings on the hour, but the connections have shorted out. The record turns and turns, but over the speakers comes incoherent noise.

The archaic religious rhetoric in which the churches have isolated themselves, has become dysfunctional. At times it sounds positively obscene. The words which once—in times when the sense of the sacred was still shared—called forth the Spirit, have changed into soporific sound-clusters, that produce an agreeable numbness, a churchy stupor. They have become tranquilizers, analgesics against life-pain, antidotes against self-confrontation. Politicians use them as bugle calls, but for innumerable people, including almost all the young, religious oratory is now an irritant that causes allergies, nausea, spiritual hives, and asthma. We have developed antibodies against this language, acquired a protective deafness, akin to that against television commercials.

Names such as God, Christ, Allah, and Buddha have become fetishes behind which still shines eternal light, but too long have clerics caught their impenetrable shadows and sold them as highest truth. When Meister Eckhart, the thirteenth-century German mystic, spoke of Godhead, when Nagarjuna, in second-century India experienced "The Void," Sunyata, these were inspirations of the spirit that pierced the shadows, but once spoken of, endlessly repeated, even these illuminations have become murky. And yet, in their murkiness I find my own baffled perceptions and most intimate intuitions clarified, confirmed.

Have not illuminations, intuitions of Reality, always been expressed in words and gestures so personal, so culture- and time-bound that they can only be decoded by those who had almost similar experiences? These glimpses of Reality that take place in the no-man's land between silence and speech, are inexpressible in language, for each revelation, every theophany is unique and ineffable. Congealed in words, all revelations are more or less equally distorted. The Nameless, once named, is no longer the true Nameless, as Lao-tzu warned us twenty-five hundred years ago. "Your ordinary mind is the Buddha," "Your daily life is the Way," "I am the Way" are words spoken on the outer rim of language uttered under the explosive pressures of insight, of revelation. Without that insight all scriptures, all revelation remain noise or printed matter, dangerous printed matter.

Can we still gain such insight without a detour via the East? What is a pilgrimage that skips the East?

The seat belt sign goes off. "No, thank you, Miss. No cocktail just now."

"Concerning that about which one cannot speak, one must keep silent," Wittgenstein tells us again and again. But surely we may gropingly stammer about what we have seen, what we have experienced, have lived, in order to offer it to others who may have experienced, lived, seen similarly. To offer it and share it, not for discussion, dissection, or debate, but for contemplation and reflection on That Which Matters, but for which we have no language.

Stammerers, mutterers, visionaries, poets, saints, fools, rather than all the brilliant theologians, philosophers, have encouraged me. They stammered, "You are not alone, you are not crazy, not crazier than I." Does this mean that perhaps the words are still intelligible, that the myths have not lost their meaning—provided they are stammered? Is it the tone of voice that speaks them, that once-born unctuous, self-assured, authoritarian, yet self-pitying pulpit drone that kills their meaning?

To dare stammer and stutter without pretension, pointing without expecting adulation for the pointing finger, inviting the disdain of the experts whose skill consists in being objective about that which is most subjective, to stammer without any other defense than, "This is my experience, this is my vision, this is how words and concepts once irreconcilable, clashing in my brain, echoed in my heart and fused easily."

Why not simply say "heart"? For "soul" still sounds old-fashioned, "psyche" ice-cold-technical, and even "spirit" sounds unctuous. Why not then "heart," the organ that resists both transplantation and demythologization? Where does a man point when he speaks of his innermost being, his deepest subjectivity and sincerity? Does he point at his belly or his head? Or does he place his hand on his chest, on that illogical, amoral, clairvoyant heart that harbors the reasons that reason itself knows nothing of, and that beats time with eternity? Here it is that the concepts that clash in the brain may fuse without fuss or bother. At its core each human heart is Sacred Heart.

Underneath, all is still ochre desert, but we must be approaching Teheran, for the stewardesses have stopped their smiling, put on their ridiculous little bowler hats, arrange their hair, critically adjust the make-up of their mating masks. We are losing altitude.

Of Teheran only an after-image remains. Grim faces of customs officials in exaggerated slow motion. Wide suburban American streets. Three baffled mountaineers in sheepskins with turbans and long moustaches trying to cross a traffic circle, where in the middle, shiny new limousines stand revolving on a platform.

Again, deep below crinkles the desert in crumpled sand patterns. Something that looks like a road ends in nowhere. Do I see water in the distance or trembling air? We cannot yet have crossed all of Iran. The plane seems to stand still in mid-air.

I read Chuang-Tzu, 500 B.C. "Am I a butterfly dreaming that I am a man, or am I a man dreaming I am a butterfly?"

This skidding of consciousness, this slipping from man to butterfly and back—Chuang-Tzu has no monopoly.

I was five and lying in high grass. A bee hummed close to my eye and frightened me. Then the bee started to suck honey and at that very moment I became sun, bee, flower and grass. "Me" had evaporated with my fear.

Then, when I was eleven, on a country road, I saw a snow flurry approach from afar. The first few snowflakes fell around my feet from the dark wintry sky. I saw how some of the flakes melted immediately on impact, others stayed. Again, Me disappeared, melted with snowflakes, became one with road and sky and snowstorm. It has happened often, always when least expected.

A few hours before leaving on this journey, driving somewhere in New Jersey, I lost my way back to the parkway. At last at a traffic light stood a pedestrian, a very fat man in a battered homburg hat. A greasy cigar stump stuck out straight from what looked more like a snout than a face.

"How do I get to Route 4?" I called out.

"Route 4," he repeated, chewing on his cigar. "Nothing to it!" His little eyes twinkled with kindness. "Take a left at the second light, can't miss it!" He had put his fat hand on my sleeve and given a friendly squeeze.

I looked at him and saw. I tried to thank him, but no sound came. I made a kind of bow. The jelly had become Man.

What is spiritual experience? A snowflake melting, a bee sucking honey, a fat man at a traffic light. Trivia.

"On your left, ladies and gentlemen, you see Bombay, and just below us the estuary of the Indus. Our speed is now 660 mph, altitude 31,000 feet. We'll land at Colombo at 2:10."

Cannot each one recall such trivia of which no one has the monopoly, these trivia that open the eye to the natural being awesomely supernatural? These touches of grace where reality opens up and we *know* that we are one with this reality, no longer estranged, but belonging, at home, here and now.

Why be so prudish, so afraid in this age of pornography, to speak of these naked moments of bliss when, liberated from the Me, in a flash of insight you glimpse your true being, your Self? Never again shall you be as ignorant as before. Your life-course changes. The Me is isolation, the Self is communal. Where we dare to share these glimpses of self without pretensions or phoniness, authentic human community is present, Now/Here.

Two sweet rolls. "Coffee or tea?" A cardboard airplane omelet, correctly tailored in London. Two neat sausages. Was the pig slaughtered in Yorkshire, or did it yell its agony in New Zealand, was it frozen, flown to Heathrow, ground up in Edgeware, to be eaten here?

On the sausage sits an Iranian fly. Its left front leg drags arthritically. As my hand moves, the fly takes off from 31,000 feet and 660 mph, orbits in the fuselage, splashes down smoothly in a thin planting of hair up front.

Women on Colombo waterfront

⚹ Sri Lanka ⚹

The prehistoric taxi from Colombo Airport rattles through the stereotyped palm groves, bougainvillea, and hovel villages of all *tristes tropiques*. Cows block the road, water buffaloes plow the fields. After the chill of ice-cold modern Teheran, Sri Lanka's air is an opaque thick, syrupy turbulence, Colombo, a compressed slum of 500,000, congested with oxcarts and senile British taxis. Girls in long-skirt dirndls and in saris sway like zinnias. Post-colonial traffic cops with RAF moustaches blow their whistles. In the narrow streets of a business district called the Fort, the scaly department stores with British names stand decaying. Then space suddenly bursts open. Left of the road, in front of the brownstone Parliament buildings stands the first prime minister of independent Sri Lanka, cast in bronze, amidst the flowers, raising a triumphal father-of-the-fatherland arm. On the right, a mile-long green parade ground, called Gall Face, is separated from the beach by a concrete esplanade. Beyond, smooth and endless lies the Indian Ocean. Freighters, as required, decorate the horizon, blow plumes of smoke into a peacock-blue sky.

At the end of the green stands a cream-colored curlicued apartment house, once imported, complete with civil servants, from Kensington. On the third floor, a sullen servant in white answers the bell. Into the Victorian mahogany drawing room, ceiling fans turning, floats sixtyish Mrs. Clarke-Walker in sugar-pink sari to bid us welcome in syncopated colonial British.

"Put that luggage down, Abraham!" she commands softly. "Abraham will look after you, just ring the bell!"

Abraham is dark-skinned, middle-aged, in a spotless white lunghi. He bows, smiles. "Good evening, Madam. Good evening, Master." He trots away, trots back, puts a halved papaya on the table. Abraham still trots, still says "Master," "Madam." How long?

"Here in Sri Lanka," says Professor G. P. Malalasekara, ex-ambassador to Russia and Great Britain, ex-representative of his country to the United Nations, Minister of Education, and a

Buddhist scholar of international reputation, "Buddhists, Hindus, Muslims, and Christians have lived in harmony for centuries. Here Buddhism is not merely a religion. It has become the creative force of our entire civilization. It has shaped our history, our literature, our art, our philosophy. Buddhism has pervaded our social and political institutions, our code of moral conduct— theoretically speaking. It was brought here in the fourth century B.C. only two hundred years after Gautama's death. Only in Sri Lanka has Theravada Buddhism retained its original purity. It instilled in people peacefulness, gentleness, tolerance, and compassion towards all that lives and breathes."

We are sitting in his cosy living room, surrounded by good modern paintings, obviously assembled for the best of reasons, personal taste.

"What is your prognosis," I ask him, "for real understanding and cooperation between Christians and Buddhists now that the institutional religions are everywhere threatened by the antireligious onslaught of a technological society?"

"I am not optimistic," he says. "The gap is too deep and wide. We Buddhists don't believe in God, consequently not in his creation of the world out of nothing, nor do we believe in the afterlife of the ego soul. We have no Saviour; the Buddha is no Saviour, never presented himself as such. He does not sacrifice himself, doesn't take the sins of all mankind upon himself. Christians project their problems on Jesus instead of solving them for themselves. The Buddha declares clearly that human beings carry the burdens of their own sins, that they have to seek liberation, emancipation through their own efforts, that no god can do it for them. His teaching is based on the understanding of the ultimate facts of life. The laws that govern life are merciless and the Buddha is far from mealy-mouthed about the facts of human existence. All existence is transitory, unsatisfactory, sorrowful, he says. But he shows the way out of suffering by the destruction of the desire that causes it. Humans are ignorant, deluded, rather than rebellious. The Buddha does not pretend to be anything but a guide who urges us to 'work out our own salvation with diligence,' encouraging us to have trust and faith in our capacity to do just that. No, the gap is too wide. We can respect one another, but I see little ground for close cooperation."

Around the ornamental clock tower at the Fort's center, the decrepit Austin taxis shriek through curves, doors fly open. On the sidewalks, under the colonnades of the Victorian law courts, in the niches of the decrepit, grandiloquent post office, in front of the run-down department stores and of Thomas Cook & Sons—the Sons are indolent Sinhalese—black marketeers in dollars lie in wait for tourists. Against the buildings hang and loiter the unemployable, the sullen young men, who together with senile cars are symbolic of every third-world country. Everyone complains of unemployment, corruption, shortage of consumer goods, national bankruptcy. Europeans who retired to spend their last years on a paradisical island are panicky prisoners, dreaming hopeless dreams of getting out. "Every penny is blocked. We are in a trap; God knows what will happen."

At dusk, in an ultramarine sky fly children's kites: dragons and black paper crows with scarlet, flapping, fluttering legs. Boys race gaunt wild-eyed ponies across the green of Gall Face, leaving trails of gold dust. On the Esplanade, near the baroque Gall Face Hotel from colonial days, saris, soft pink, pistachio, sky-blue, blow in the lazy breeze, transparent auras around the women's bodies.

Colombo's women have counted successfully on the irresistible sex-appeal of this style of implying that which an American girl in miniskirt and halter insists on showing off, until she looks fragmented, a toy for fetishists. Old couples shuffle silently in the setting sun. Men in jackets over baggy white trousers, stop and go, gesticulate in endless soundless disputation. Shabby oldsters of military bearing, bristling grey moustaches in the air, march in desperate briskness, keeping in form. In the deepening dusk, a star becomes visible. The surf hardly sighs. A grandmother in a deep mauve sari presses a child against her. The little boy, uncon-

solable, points out to sea where his mauve balloon rises higher
and higher, gone forever. It is miraculously quiet. Time has
stopped here long ago, in 1914, in 1910.

It is quite dark now. Huge, grey-necked crows gather on the
edge of the boardwalk, caw wildly, predict the inexorable
resumption of time and terror.

The stupa of Kelanya, a hundred and fifty feet high, abruptly
rises up out of the dusty foliage like a gigantic, dead-white
breast. Small figures move clockwise around it. The stupa is the
spiritual core of a typical Buddhist temple, an architectural complex that comprises an "image house," living quarters for the
monks, preaching halls, and of course a Bodhi-tree. The stupa,
which usually contains a relic, is a stylization of a honorific para-
sol or canopy, or perhaps of a stylized sepulchral mount, or perhaps a symbol of the cosmos. Opinions differ. The Bodhi-tree,
ficus religiosus, is the tree under which Gautama sat in meditation
when he attained Enlightenment, Nirvana, and thus became the
Buddha, teacher of that Middle Way between the extremes of
self-indulgence and ascetic self-torture which must lead to the
supreme insight, to the peace that passeth understanding, to the
Wisdom that is Compassion and vice versa.

Kelanya Raja Maha Vihara is the oldest temple of Colombo, centuries older than the city itself, according to legend, founded at
the time Gautama Buddha paid his three visits to the island. The
gigantic reclining Buddha of Kelanya, some thirty feet long, lies
in the hushed dusky shell of the image house, his serene massive
head supported by the right hand. The eyes that were clearly
half open when seen from a distance, seem to close miraculously
as I get near the radiant peacefulness of the face. The uninterrupted film of imagination and thought is suddenly stalled in
this presence, this cosmic, transcendent Image of Humanness.
Men, women, and children bring on their joined hands offerings
of lotus blossoms, symbolic of the transiency of all life. The stone
bench at the immense Buddha's feet is covered with the fading

flowers. The devout raise joined hands above their heads, then kneel, bow down until arms and forehead touch the floor.

Our driver has followed us into the temple. He bows down deeply, stands motionless, his hands folded.

"Are you a Buddhist?"

"No, Sah, I am a Catholic."

Being a good Catholic, he makes an unscheduled stop at Santa Lucia, a Roman Catholic church, kneels at the altar, as if to reassure Saint Anthony, Santa Lucia, and the Virgin of his loyal love. He kisses the fingers of both his hands, touches each statue. Then he rushes off across the stinking, crowded fish market.

I find a fine ten-year-old Ford for the trip to Rajarata, the "Land of Kings" around Anuradhapura and Polonnaruwa. My driver is a thin, dignified, aristocratically distant Muslim named Hussan. I never find out where he eats or sleeps. He disappears discreetly, but is always waiting at the car when needed.

Plump monks in yellow robes, walking along the road, carry begging bowl and fan. Younger monks, a step behind them, hold umbrellas over their heads.

"They eat only two meals a day," says Hussan, "but look how fat they are! You know why, Sah? Because they are happy! They are happy, for they have the easy life. I wonder why not all boys become monks, anyone can become a monk, rich or poor."

The narrow road to Kandy winds between walls of jungle. Wobbling bamboo bridges span the deep gully of a stream that gradually widens into a river. Children and water buffaloes splash about in the brown water. The buffaloes' massive horned heads stare into the sun in bovine ecstasy. Occasionally they move a hind leg and scoop water over their horns, making them glisten like polished bronze. Boys throw stones at large bats that hang asleep in the trees. The bats wake up, flutter around helplessly in the blinding light, shriek in panic.

The Temple of the Tooth, the holiest shrine of Sri Lanka, is a rambling complex that lies on a hillock overlooking placid Kandy Lake. In the chiaroscuro of the antechamber men in white sarongs, blood-red scarves around their naked torsos, beat drums. Above the drumbeats rises obsessively a flute. Pilgrims carry flower offerings bought from a stall outside, kneel down in solitary prayer. Women lift up their babies to the Buddha. A square locked room at the top of an ornamental staircase contains the Buddha's tooth. It is a fake. The original one, centuries ago, was *Ad Majorem Dei Gloriam* crushed to bits by a Portuguese bishop, who should have known that a relic is only as holy as human reverence has made it. We join the line to circumambulate the venerable, phony bicuspid.

The Mahayanake of Malwatta, the Buddhist bishop who wields spiritual authority over southern Sri Lanka, lives in a monastery across the lake. He is the successor to the eighteenth-century monks imported from Thailand to resume ordinations after decades of war had decimated the monastic population. Boys, who bum cigarettes, guide me to the Mahayanake's run-down monastery. The frail, toothless octogenarian in his faded ochre habit is so deaf that he understands only half my shouted questions. But he mumbles his monologue, punctuated by shakes of his shaven bony head.

"Since the West," he says, "is losing some of its conceit, perhaps we can at last be brought closer together. It may be able to see now that Buddhism is a teaching that looks into life, not merely at its surface. The Buddha's doctrine rests on the idea of 'knowing reality as it is.' He is a guide to us. The doctrine helps us to get rid of the ills of life, to know what truly human conduct consists of. But don't call it an ethical system, for morality is only the beginning, not the end of Buddhism. Its end is enlightenment."

While he speaks I draw him. He does not pay attention, but two young monks eye every stroke with amused awe.

the Mahayanake of Malwatta.

On the road to Polonnaruwa, at Katugustota, a few miles from
Kandy, elephants are bathing. The mahouts have spotted our car
long before it hobbles down to the river's edge. They prod their
animals, come trotting up the bank. Suddenly it is pitch-dark.
The car is caught between dripping, grey elephant flanks on port
and starboard. One of the mahouts, invisible, demands rupees in
a strident countertenor. In panic we throw banknotes out of the
window. The walls of skin at once start moving. The grinning
bandits ride their huge mounts back into the water, without
another glance in our direction.

The Parakrama Sea is a six-thousand-acre artificial lake close to
Polonnaruwa, one of those astonishing "tanks" that are part of
the incredibly sophisticated irrigation system interconnected by
carefully graded canals, built some nine centuries ago in Sri
Lanka's Golden Age. Anuradhapura had been the capital for
nearly a thousand years, but it became too vulnerable to the
invasions by the Cholas from southern India when its protective
wildernesses had disappeared and the jungles had either
become cultivated or destroyed in the internecine struggles for
royal succession. It was finally sacked early in the eleventh century. Polonnaruwa's moment of glory as capital of Sri Lanka
had come.

On the sloping meadow with purple and yellow flowers, I
nearly step on a three-foot-long lizard. His prehistoric head
pulses with life. Squirrel-gray monkeys with keen black faces
play in the shadowless glare of noon. Against the light stands
the Gal Vihara, a rock wall in which three gigantic Buddha
images have been hewn. The Buddha sits here in contemplation,
he stands more than forty feet high preaching the Dharma, lies
peacefully on his side in Paranirvana, in death. Sudden noise
explodes the stillness. From nowhere, in sweatshirts, sailors' hats
and jeans, three Fellini clowns appear, laughing and shouting in
French. Frantically they photograph one another against the

sacred backdrop, their movie cameras rattle like machine guns. "Fantastique!" yells the female clown in mini-shorts, dancing a jig on top of the dead Buddha.

On the outskirts of the holy city of Anuradhapura, 1,840 steps lead to the ruined cave monastery of Mihintale, founded about 250 B.C. by the Indian monk Mahinda, son of Emperor Asoka, who came to Sri Lanka with his followers. From here Buddhism spread over Sri Lanka like a tidal wave.

The heart of Anuradhapura, as holy a city as Jerusalem, Benares, or Mecca, is a decrepit tree on iron crutches, protected by a golden fence, within high walls. It may well be the oldest tree in the world, this shoot of the very Bodhi-tree under which, in Buddh-Gaya near Benares, Gautama had attained the awakening that made him into the Buddha. The tree was brought to Anuradhapura, already an old city when it became Sri Lanka's capital in 300 B.C., by the royal nun Sanghamitta, Mahinda's sister. Hundreds of faded red and blue flags wave among the thin foliage. Monks chant and gesture over small clusters of humanity, babies being consecrated to the Buddha at the sacred fence. Kneeling pilgrims touch the gold railing in adoration. A family of twenty, from grandmothers to babies, squeeze themselves out of a dented yellow minibus, pour oil in a long row of iron votive lamps, light them, and pose stiffly for their photograph in this holy of holies. The women bring flower offerings to the gold fence and to the stone shrines all around. On the steps of one of these, a young German couple sit eating sandwiches, their backs turned to the Buddha inside. An old woman in a dark sari demonstratively kneels in front of them, her face in the dust. Shocked, they stuff their sandwiches in a rucksack, slink away. A stocky man of forty interrupts my drawing.

"My name is Pereira. I am a civil servant and merchant," he announces cryptically. "You are no ordinary tourist, are you?" he questions me, pointing at my drawing.

"No, perhaps I am not quite a tourist, more a pilgrim like yourselves." It takes some explaining. He takes off to report, obviously impressed and satisfied. His family, worship ended, has started to picnic in a far corner of the courtyard.

The Isuruminya Vihara, the complex of rock temples where Mahinda lies buried, overlooks a charming pond. Lovely bas-reliefs of secular subjects, of a horse and rider, of lovers in tender embrace, of an elephant, are carved in the rock wall. A tourist bus stops. Forty Swedes rush through the sacred space, looking for lavatories. Girls take one another's picture with lovers and Buddhas as background.

In the courtyard I draw two monks, grimly discussing the invasion, eyeing the half-naked blond girls in shorts and miniskirts. We pretend not to notice each other. Then one of them says, "Drawing is hard work. You are seeing. Those others just take snapshots and forget."

In the hot afternoon sun I stand in front of the Samadhi Buddha, . who has sat here in bliss ever since the fourth century. I try to draw, but it is just too hot. There is nothing wrong with my model. His curiously Semitic profile reminds me of a psychoanalyst of my acquaintance and from him my thoughts drift to Freud. How would Gautama have expressed himself in post-Freudian terms? He would have approved of Freud's,"Where id was, there shall be ego." He never denied the development of ego, of social identity, as being essential. But it is only half the fulfillment of human destiny.

Gautama might have said, "Where id was there shall be ego, where ego has been achieved, there it shall be transcended, ego has to be broken through."

He might not have said "destroyed." He might have counseled, "Recognize your narcissism, monks. Be conscious of it, eradicate it."

Hussan thinks he knows a shortcut to Aukana. Soon we are lost in a maze of palm-lined dusty roads, cross the deep overflow of a "tank," a quiet, wide waterfall, then get stuck between rice paddies. In the tanks women are bathing, chastely covered by long cotton shirts. White herons sail low over the water, splashing children wave at the car. The island is here disquietingly paradisical, it makes one think of Aldous Huxley's *The Island*, an oasis of tranquillity and goodness lying under impending doom.

At Aukana, the Pereiras' battered yellow bus has stopped at the foot of a high hill. The whole clan is climbing up to the sanctuary, the grandmother is pushed and pulled up the rocky steps. The Aukana Buddha shoots up, a stone flame, into the evening sky. From the hillock across from the immense statue it looks dematerialized, a pure manifestation of the Spirit in its immeasurable dimensions. Women, at the immense feet, tiny dwarfs, take flowers out of plastic bags, sprinkle them with rose water, place them on an altar, prostrate themselves.

Hardly have I started to draw, when a young heavy-set monk appears from nowhere. His round shaven head is almost black. I ask him to stand still so that I can make him part of my drawing, but he must talk, must give the foreigner an idea of what this Buddha, what Buddhism is about. He gets more excited as monosyllabic answers show that I am not a total stranger to his subject. Our conversation then becomes a friendly dispute on Theravada and Mahayana Buddhism. With Buddhists such disputes have a way of remaining light and good-humored, merely touching on verities and realizations, without any compulsion to define, convince, convert. They intend mutual revelation and stimulation rather than verbal victory. Reconciled to reality, one either shares the inexpressible with one who already knows, or is content to whisper the unteachable to the deaf.

"Our ideal is to become an Ahrat, to succeed in reaching enlightenment by meditation," says the monk.

"That is Theravada, of course. My own sympathies are drawn to the Bodhisattva, the ideal of Mahayana, the Great Vehicle. The Ahrat enters into the bliss of Nirvana. But the Bodhisattva at the point of enlightenment refuses to enter. He has vowed to forgo

"Where ego has been achieved, let it be transcended."

this bliss as long as a single creature remains unredeemed, unliberated, enslaved to delusion and ignorance. He turns back, descends into the marketplace in order to bestow blessings on all men. He uses his attainment of self-nature, of the fullness of human potentiality in order to reawaken hope, to encourage us, give us hope of reaching our own fullest potential, thus bringing salvation to all."

"The Bodhisattva," I add, "is the supreme artist, for 'art is that which despite all, gives hope!'"

"You are a heretic!" he says with a big smile.

The Pereira family has gathered around us, listens, scans our faces, although Pereira Senior is the only one who understands English. He nods gravely at whatever is said by the monk or me. Dusk envelops our little group. The immense body of the Buddha—hewn out of the rock by giants, according to the legend—is already wrapped in mauve veils, but the last rays of the sun set the face aglow, encompassing us all in the smile of his supreme Sanity.

It is time to leave. We greet one another with folded hands. The monk stays on the promontory and waves.

"Come back! Come back soon!" he cries.

We stop and turn and wave again and again.

"Do come back!" he cries.

The Aukana Buddha's body has disappeared in darkness, but the divine smile is still visible in the night sky.

Is the face of the Aukana Buddha that of the "Christ in Glory" of Autun, of Vézelay? If Christian theological debate through the centuries had taken place under the image of the Transfigured Christ instead of under the crucifix, would Western history have been less arid, less bitter, less bloody?

On the dark road the car passes a procession of covered oxcarts, tiny oil lamps swing between wooden wheels. Around campfires people are cooking their meals at the roadside.

the Aukana Buddha.

Hussan talks about the religious tolerance of the Sinhalese. He himself, although a Muslim, goes every Wednesday night to the novena at All Saints Church.

"Why?" I ask.

"Because of the vows! Because of the vows! We all go there, Catholics, Muslims, Buddhists, just for the vows!"

I don't understand. But Hussan can't explain. I ask Mr. Clarke-Walker about these mysterious vows. He is sixty, pale, faintly Cockney.

"Oh well, that's common here. The missus does it too. But, of course, she is very religious, very religious. It is this way, you see." My host goes on to explain, "People go to All Saints where they have this miraculous Virgin, don't you know. She is all encrusted with jewels and such and they ask her favors and then they vow to do this or that, don't you know, for instance to pray to her so many times every day or week, or to go to church so and so often, or they pledge to give her some money, that is, if she delivers what they are praying for, and so on and so forth. Maud believes in all this, she has what they call faith. When I was sick for instance, I had this thing, diverticulitis, a bloody bore, and the surgeon, top man here, said we'd better go in there now, in ten years time you'll be seventy. So he cut me open and everything went fine, except that on the table I turned a bit blue and my eyes rolled up. He just happened to look. So he took a scalpel and slit my throat. I came to, kind of, and all was fine. And then, damn it, he sees me turn blue again. So he just ripped the stitch out and the matron put a tube into me. Well, when they told Maud she passed out cold. And then she got everybody to pray for me, don't you know, the nuns and priests and even the Buddhist monks. There were more bloody monks and fathers and sisters around me than doctors and nurses. She made all kinds of vows to this Lady of Perpetual Help and so on and so forth. But don't you see, it wasn't really any use, it came afterwards anyway!"

In All Saints' Annex, next door to Father Herat's office, little boys are practicing brass instruments. Father Herat, white-haired and

distinguished, with un-Sinhalese energy in every one of his movements, tells me he is a convert from Buddhism, in fact that some of
his brothers are Buddhist monks. I ask, "How is the relationship
between the Catholic and Buddhist clergy?"

"None," he says, "except that on official occasions we sit on
the grandstand together. The Buddhist monks think they have
all the answers. Most of them are rogues."

He should know.

He proudly shows me issues of his "Novena News" and of his
best-selling rotogravures of Our Lady of Perpetual Help in both
the individual and family size.

"I sell them by the hundreds," he says, "Muslims, Parsis sneak
in and give me 500, 600 rupees hidden under a book."

People walk into the office, interrupt us humbly, hand Father
envelopes with petitions to the Virgin and money. He smiles at
them, "There is always room for more!"

At last he frees himself for a guided tour, "Here is our new
carillon. Look, 37 bells, each one inscribed with its own name! It
plays the Marian hymn every hour on the hour!" We walk over
to the giftshop-snackbar with its collection of rosaries.

"These are our cheapest, you see, but look at these beautiful
imported ones—a lot of trouble getting them now with all those
currency restrictions. You must have a taste of our baked goods,
I am very proud of them!"

A smiling nun in rimless glasses hands me a pastry.

"Excellent, Father, delicious!"

"And here, this is our free clinic, here we distribute the medicines. You see, the fact that the medicines come from us helps a
lot. No, no, we have no doctor. Sister here gives them the medicines. Really bad cases? She sends them off to the hospital."

The new marble altar, I agree, is splendid indeed.

"It's really a shame," Father says, "the old one was mag-ni-fi-
cent. What can you do? We had to turn the altar around, of
course. Don't ask what it cost!"

The church is immaculate.

"Believe it or not, I have to paint at least once a year," says

Father. "Those candles make a terrible mess! It's the non-Catholics. Let's assume they burn ten candles to get a favor. They are not like our Catholics. They never quite trust us, so they wait until every single candle has burned all the way to the end! Can you imagine? It is filthy black here in no time! I just have to keep painting."

An expensively dressed, squat woman appears in the doorway, gesticulates in obvious distress. Father Herat folds his hands and cries, "Ah, there you are at last. I have been so worried about you!" He excuses himself, whispers, "An emergency! Make yourself comfortable in my office! Have a look at the testimonials in Novena News."

I read:

"Dearest Mother,

I am to be fixed up for tomorrow, i.e. on the 1st September. I have decided to ask for a salary of Rs. 100. Instill into the hearts of the management and grant me this last favour, as I know that You have done so much for me and that You would not hesitate to do more for me. I promise, dearest Mother, that with the first salary I will offer You my thanks and pay You my respects.

That night I dream that I am dead. I see myself die. I try to speak to people I have known, to friends who surround my corpse. I can't remember their names. I hear them say, "He is dead." I feel vaguely that my shape has changed, I now have the shape of an eye. Wandering around I see others who are dead, wandering as I am. Enclosed in my eye-shaped bubble I cannot make contact. I ask myself if I am really dead. I look into a mirror at my eyes. They are turned up, absolutely dead, remind me of poached eggs. I am filled with indescribable terror. But in this terror I suddenly remember that if I had died, I should have seen a flash of the Clear Light. Let me try and think—have I seen the flash of Clear Light? I would remember that! I have not! I have not seen that flash, so I cannot have died! I have been cheated! I have cheated myself! I shoot up as from the bottom of a deep well and wake up. I awaken Claske.

"I have been dead," I say. I ask, "Do I look dead?"

She turns on the light and the fan, puts her hands on my face, kisses me. At that very moment the fuse blows. Through the window I see the starry sky; still alive, I am calm as a lake. For how long?

I tell the dream to Narada Mahathera. He says, "You had a spiritual rebirth."

Narada, in his seventies, is one of the most distinguished Buddhist scholars of Sri Lanka. When I first met him in his threadbare saffron-yellow habit, I took him for a working monk in the monastery of which he is the abbot. His manner is as unassuming as his appearance, but he radiates quiet authority.

"Buddhism as well as Christianity is based on fear," he explains, "on fear of the unknown. Buddhism is homocentric, Christianity is theocentric. Buddhism is introverted, Christianity is extroverted."

"To me Christo-centricity is at the same time homocentric and theocentric," I interject. "Christology is an anthropology, just as Buddhology is an anthropology. Both deal with the deepest, truest, essential nature of man. Both Christ and Buddha to me are the living, incarnate criteria of what it really means to be human. Does this sound unacceptable to you?"

He cocks an eyebrow and gestures for me to continue.

"As far as Buddhism's introversion is concerned, by itself I find that of no merit. If it is not balanced by extroversion towards the world, it leaves the world in its mess. If humans are worthy of being enlightened, they are worthy of being fed! Buddhism seems to be lacking a social ethic; it seems all too unconcerned with social justice, with the needs of concrete human beings. What you call Christian extroversion on the other hand, has indeed the tendency to become a meddlesome paternalistic activism, unaware of the need for a profound self-examination—I mean examination of what self really is—and so it makes the world's mess even messier. Do you see any chance of integration of Christian and Buddhist values and meanings, Narada Mahathera? Could not Eastern introversion and Western activism complement one another? Isn't it high time for a synthesis?"

"The differences are too fundamental! Better leave Christianity Christianity and Buddhism Buddhism! First there is your Judeo-Christian God. When I was once lecturing in a church in London I was asked about our Buddhist denial of God. I answered, 'How could I, sitting under the very roof of God, have the discourtesy to deny him?' But as you know, we reject the idea of a personal God who created the world *ex nihilo* and is to be feared and obeyed. Hence the exclusive sonship of Christ makes no sense to us at all, neither his role as Savior of an immortal soul, for we do not believe man has an immortal ego-soul.

"The Buddha does not pretend to be a savior. He is the teacher who exhorts his disciples to depend on themselves in order to reach liberation. He does not condemn men by calling them wretched sinners, but he gladdens them by showing that they are potentially pure in heart."

"Isn't there here a parallel to the Christian 'glad tidings'?" I asked. "Jesus shows in his words and especially in his manner of life and death, his fullest acceptance of what you call karma. He demonstrates the full potentiality of man, the kingdom that is within."

"Christ is a Saviour," he insisted vehemently. "To believe in him is to achieve salvation. Nobody is saved by believing in the Buddha. A man is saved by following his teachings, by living the Dharma, by living according to the law of reality, of the truth. Buddhism does not deal in superstitious rites and ceremonies, dogmas, sacrifices, and repentance as the price of salvation. Repentance is simply the will not to repeat one's foolishness. The teaching of Buddha, the Dharma, is grounded in factual reality. Buddhism is a philosophical and ethical system which our human experience can verify as being in accord with reality. It neither violates conscience nor intelligence. It leaves thought free, is without fanaticism, and does not know persecution."

I tried, "Many contemporary Christians would not object to a formulation that would run approximately: God is the very ground of my Being. God equals the ultimate reality. If I may use my own private language: God is the very Structure of Reality. I see the Christ as the one who discerns the Structure of Reality, recognizes it within himself as his ground, as his deepest self, and who empties himself of the delusional ego."

"Buddhism denies the reality of the ego. There is no *atman*, no self," Narada said severely.

"That is not the whole of Buddhism, is it?" I objected. "That is Theravada. Mahayana does not see the self as mere illusion. The True Self, according to this view, is the empirical psychological self, but minus its egocentric, narcissistic delusions. The True Self, after this discounting of ego, is as rich in content as ever before, even immensely richer, because it no longer stands pitted against the world but contains the world within itself. *Anatta* (litt. the 'absence of *atman*') according to this view, means that there is no psychological substratum corresponding to the word *self*. May I continue? Christ lives his identification with his Ground, with the Structure of Reality to the point where he can call it father. 'I and the Father are one.' He manifests this supreme insight in his compassionate love, his agape that he pours impartially on the just and the unjust."

"You give an extremely Buddhist interpretation of Christianity. Or a Christian interpretation of Buddhism! You would have trouble selling it at All Saints! Do you practice meditation?"

"In my own way. I can't sit cross-legged and I feel I don't have to. It would be unnatural for me. Unnecessary," I answered.

"It isn't absolutely necessary. So what is your way?"

"My way is simply seeing. When I see an ox and I draw that ox, I become this ox and I see, I realize, the mystery of creatureliness, of impermanence in it and in me. We become equivalent in our condition of creatureliness. While I am drawing a hunchback or an old woman, they become as beautiful for me as an athlete or a lovely girl. When I draw a tree or the children on their ponies in the sunset on Gall Face, I see their transiency. I see that they, the tree, the children, the ponies, and I, must die. I do not look-at; I see!"

Narada nodded and said, "To come back to Christ. If you are right, how could he say, 'My God, my God, why hast thou forsaken me?'"

"That was not the risen Christ speaking, that was still Jesus before his task was fulfilled. But at the end he says, 'It is finished, consummated. Into thy hands I commend my Spirit.' Hui-Neng says, 'One thought of enlightenment and one is a Buddha, one unenlightened thought and one is a common man.'"

"That is a Mahayana view again," he said in a tone of slight reproof. "Jesus was no Buddha. He was a Bodhisattva. Although when he said, 'They know not what they do,' he sounds like a Buddha."

"You mentioned superstitious ceremonies and rites. Can't one see these rites instead as *upaya* (skillful means, stratagems) used to reach people on their diverse levels of understanding, of consciousness? I have seen many people pray in front of Buddha images since I came here."

"That is not Buddhism; they are uneducated people. It is popular religion," he brushed it aside.

"But they consider themselves Buddhists and you accept them as such," I insisted.

"Buddhism does not condemn easily. In this temple I see women praying to the Buddha to give them back husbands who have run away. Then one smiles. They also pray for favors from the *devas* who they believe inhabit the Bo-tree and these *devas* may have a certain relative degree of reality."

"But this relative degree of reality of divine beings you consider as a mere construct of the human mind, do you not?"

"Yes, indeed."

"Like Our Lady of Perpetual Help?"

He smiled, "Ah, the Virgin is an exceptionally powerful *deva* and a very profitable one! But, of course, she has very able helpers in bestowing her favors. Some of the jobs people pray for are provided by the influence-peddling of the priests. It has been all over the papers! We do not encourage superstition; we neither promote nor exploit people's ignorance. As to mature Buddhists, when confronted with the Buddha image, they pay reverence to what the image represents. If mature Buddhists offer flowers and incense to an image, they makes themselves feel that they are in the presence of the living Buddha and draw inspiration from his noble personality and his boundless compassion. The Bo-tree is no magical object, but a symbol of enlightenment. These external objects are in no way indispensable, they are merely useful to help concentrate one's attention.

"Buddhism is a teaching that looks into life instead of at it. As a guide to conduct based on insight that enables us to confront life with fortitude and death with serenity, Buddhism is truly a religion. The Dharma, the doctrine of reality, shows the way to our deliverance from suffering. Whether Buddhas arise or not, the Dharma exists, hidden from our ignorant eyes, until an Enlightened One, a Buddha, reveals it to us. This Dharma is not something outside, apart from oneself; it is inseparably related to oneself."

I thought, "If I speak of Structure of Reality and he speaks of Dharmakaya, the Body of the Law that rules the universe, couldn't we be speaking of the same thing or of something analogous? And that which is not something apart from oneself, couldn't that be the kingdom within, the very core of humanness?" But I said, "One more question! Doesn't the doctrine of karma in your view enclose us in a cut-and-dried determinism? 'By their fruits you shall know them. One reaps what one sows,' are Christian expressions of the recognition of cause and effect."

He said, "If your question implies: is one bound to all one has sown and in the same proportions, let the Buddha answer, 'If anyone says that we must reap *according to* our deeds, then there would be no opportunity for the extinction of sorrow, no religious life. But if we reap *in accord with* our deeds, then religious life opens up and the extinction of *dukkha,* sorrow.' Free will (although in Buddhism the will too is dependent in its origin on conditioning) can create fresh karma. In this life I mold my future. Karma therefore has a certain plasticity. It can be formed by my creative will. Insight overcomes karma. According to Theravada Buddhism there is no God, no allover purpose in the universe, no creation, but a cyclic ebb and flood of universes. A human being, any sentient being, is a series of connected psychosomatic events, point-moments, governed by karmic law."

"Karmic law cannot be proven, can it? In that respect it is very much like God's providence, divine justice."

"It is a point of faith, but also of observation," Narada said a bit sourly.

"Could you say something about the idea of transcendence in Theravada Buddhism?"

"There is Nibbana (Nirvana). The Udana sutra says, 'There is a not-born, not-become, not-created, not-formed. If there were not this not-born, not-become, not-created, not-formed, then an escape from the born, the become, the created, the formed could not be known.'"

I leave Narada Mahathera loaded with his books, ranging from pamphlets to 700-page volumes on the intricacies of Buddhist philosophy, much to the pleasure of Qantas, TWA, and JAL who classify such items as excess baggage.

I walk back to the Fort, see karma carved in the faces of children and oldsters on the broken sidewalks, see it in my own face reflected in a windowpane. What are we but leaves on the tree called humanity? What I call "Me," what is it but this given, this psychosomatic coincidence imbedded in endless concentric circles of collectiveness: biosphere, animal kingdom, humanity, ethnic group, family. All modes and stages and combinations of living matter survive in this "Me," in this given. Yet we perceive and label ourselves and others as Sinhalese, Dutch, American, Scotch-Irish, according to some single fleeting constellation in our inextricable origins in a community of beings extending back to the beginning of life on earth.

And yet within this ironclad, eugenically and culturally conditioned given of "Me," of the human individual, there lives that ultimate mystery, that Ingredient X which is not-born, not-become, not-created, which is creative and free and demands our being aware of it, whether it is called the "unborn" or "indwelling spirit" or "Buddha Nature." Whatever it is, it is not a figment of the imagination, this Ingredient X, for it manifests itself in our spiritual antennae that pick it up. We recognize and venerate it, when mysteriously, rarely, it has incarnated itself, radiant in pure form in a Buddha, a Christ.

It is this Ingredient X which constitutes our specifically human dignity, our hope of liberation from the collective karma, it is our organ for authentic spiritual life.

It may be this Ingredient X that emboldens me to write this down, now.

India

✢ Madras ✢

During the hour of flying from Colombo to Madras a Hindu engineer tells me he is going home. There are rumors of a Maoist plot in Sri Lanka. A month later the unemployable young, college-trained for nonexistent jobs, riot. Thousands of young people, revolutionary or not, are killed off like vermin by the police. As usual, karma, rising relentlessly from its collective abyss, strikes the unsuspecting.

Against an eclectic backdrop of British cricket fields, rice paddies, dungheaps, modern factories, and elegant office blocks, stand the teeming sub-hovels of the destitute, assemblages of jute, leaves, and sheets of dirty plastic. Madras.

The first voices whisper in my ear in peculiar staccato-coloratura Indian English, hands wave persuasively at me, offering astronomical black-market rates for my dollars.

Indian hands, emaciated or pudgy, have a kinesis all their own, flutter everywhere in velocities of expressiveness that make Sicilian hands seem lazy, inarticulate memories.

Indian eyes inescapable, magnificently alive, demand to be noticed, bore into mine. Eyes superbly busy with the business of perceiving, appraising, demanding food, extorting recognition, love, pity. Often these Indian eyes are wild, crazed like those of horses in panic. The eyes of waiters, shoeshine boys, strollers, bus drivers, and lepers are alert and keen. Uninterruptedly they register, assess, assert, judge, command, implore, and take possession. The tired, unseeing, grey haddock eyes of Western cities do not exist here. These devouring eyes I see all day. I see them seeing.

At the Dasaprakash Hotel, large, Indian, Victorian, and vegetarian, the crowded balconies overhang the inner courtyard, a neglected miniature jungle. Doors stand open, Indian families lounge on beds, visiting friends squat on the floors. Wafts of movie-Indian music from radios jingle through hot, thick, sweetish air. The spastic elevator operator, the waiters, all move in grotesque slow motion, but the cockroaches in the bathroom nimbly race for shelter.

An inkling of Madras.

A hundred yards from the Dasaprakash on Poonamalle High Road a concrete bridge crosses the Cooum River. This is a respectable river running through a commercial and residential neighborhood with a Methodist Church that looks as if imported from Bournemouth. But as I walk across the bridge, the outer marshes of the Cooum reveal themselves as covered by a city of sheds, shanties, hovels of incredible misery, built of barrels, crates, leaves, tarpaper, truck bodies. On the edge of an open sewer naked children caked with dirt are playing. Crows and buzzards hover over piles of rubbish and burnt-out coal, where women sift muck through their fingers, picking bits, pieces, particles still fit for the recyclings of destitution. Madras, I am told, knows little poverty. "Wait until you see Bombay, Calcutta, Delhi!"

Close to San Thomé Cathedral in Mylapore (where according to legend Saint Thomas Didymus, the apostle, preached the gospel and was martyred) stands the Kapaleswara Temple with its *gopuram*, the immensely high sculpture-saturated entrance porch, that rises in typical south Indian style above the teeming poverty-stricken slum. At the entrance, shoes are given in safekeeping. On socks I wade through the muck of the courtyard followed by a retinue of small fry. A herd of forty middle-aged Bavarians in lederhosen and flowered dirndls stand aghast, a phalanx of fat, besieged by swarms of skinny, begging children. A blind man led by an urchin, stops, turns his milk-blue pupils at the alien presence. Two self-appointed guides, emaciated eleven- or twelve-year-olds, cannot be shaken off. Already they have the faces of pimps who have seen too much human vice from too close by. The smaller one runs off and returns with half a coconut and a banana.

A tiny girl in faded red rags tugs with uninterrupted tenacity at my trousers, picks at my sleeves, her hard black eyes, imploring, reproachful, try to catch mine. I shake her off with abrupt jerks. The tugging stops for a split second, continues as before. I try to buy her off, give her a coin. She looks at it, closes it into her tiny dirty fist, continues her tugging, suddenly assisted by five other tots.

The dank temple smells of incense and cat's urine. In a recess stands a primitive horrifying shape, unrecognizably blackened by dirt and soot. One of the guides gestures to hold out my hands. He pours coconut milk over them, then puts the coconut and half the banana on the stone slab beneath the thing. I must eat the other half. I refuse. Better go. Outside the *gopuram* the shoekeeper has disappeared with my shoes. There are no taxis. On socks I pick my way through India.

"You must speak with N. Sri Ram when you get to Madras," Narada Mahathera had insisted to my surprise, for I somehow thought of the Theosophical Society—of which N. Sri Ram is the president—as something all too Western. The Society was founded in New York in 1875 by a retired American colonel, Henry Steel Olcott and a Russian noble lady of mystical accomplishment, Helena Petrovna Blavatsky. Its purpose was "to form a nucleus of universal brotherhood of humanity without distinction of race, creed, sex, caste, color, to encourage the study of comparative religion and to investigate unexplained laws of nature and the powers latent in man." It had lost much of its original dynamism, made one think of fastidious drawing rooms, where devout elderly ladies fawn over some turbaned speaker, until the recent interest in Oriental thought gave it a new lease on life.

The taxi takes the boulevard along the marina, the splendid beach that is Madras' pride. It crosses a bridge over the Adayar River. Hundreds of men stand in the murky water washing bloomers, sheets, saris, shirts. The pale green outer marshes are covered by square miles of drying laundry as by a gigantic multicolored flag.

The headquarters of the Society, a vanilla yellow painted ghost from the turn of the century, stands at the end of a shady avenue in its own vast park. In the lobby across shiny black and

N. Sri Ram

white marble tiles, barefoot elderly ladies shuffle, bowing and smiling at one another. The hall encompasses a distinguished spiritual company in bas-relief. Moses, in person, represents Judaism; Jesus knocks at the door; Buddha sits on his lotus throne; Mohavira, the founder of Jainism, is present with his harmless swastika; Lao-tzu advertises yin and yang; Nanak, the prophet of Sikhism; Zarathustra; Minerva; ten avatars of Vishnu; Confucius; and the symbols of Shinto, Mithras, Ishtar, and Quetzalcoatl are brotherly united under thick coats of shiny vanilla paint. In niches and recesses the greats of theosophy are enshrined in marble and bronze rigor mortis. In an adjoining room, cabinets full of their medals, scrolls, plaques, diplomas, honorary degrees, and decorations are displayed. A white-haired lady on a cane shows me into the president's room.

It is almost dark. From behind a roll-top desk a tall, thin, very old man in a white robe rises slowly. His long hair falls like a snow-white silky shawl over a narrow skull of finely carved bone, the eyes are still bright and luminous, but the hand he offers is almost fleshless.

"Of course I remember Narada, a great thinker!" he says in a brittle whisper.

"Narada Mahathera is not very optimistic about an understanding between Buddhism and Christianity," I say. "What is your feeling?"

"There must be more than understanding. We simply must realize the fundamental oneness of religious experience and insight. Look at the young! Isn't it pitiful to watch their search for some modicum of truth in the inextricable web of lies of the politicians, in the delusional systems of the technologists? This world is so sick. We try to escape it. We fly to the moon—that is of course admirable, heroic—but we shan't meet our truth there either. We are born without knowing who we are, without knowing what it is to be human. The truth of what we are, where does one meet that? It may come to one in the most unlikely places, often without any particular search, just by being open to it. Wherever it comes, it always comes to the individual. It is a terrible delusion to think that it could be a collective experience. It is the individual, always and only the individual, realizing itself, who finds the truth about human nature. Community is important, but the realization that makes community possible can only come to the person, can only be experienced in the individual."

"What is your prognosis for the future of Christianity, Sri Ram?"

"One cannot speak about Christianity. There are the words and the life of Christ and then there are the Protestant Church and the Catholic Church with their paraphernalia. Always that fatal tendency to power and to paraphernalia, how immensely strong it is! The young at last repudiate the paraphernalia and the institutions which are so proud of them. But the fundamental problem remains: How to awaken the human in human beings?"

"What do you think of the new currents in the Catholic Church?"

"I find there a real effort to rediscover spiritual truth, to look beyond the paraphernalia, even beyond the dogmatic formulations. Yet there is a great danger that what is truly religious, truly spiritual, will become overpowered by over-intellectualization or by the preaching of a purely social gospel. There is danger of losing sight of the great mysteries, the intimations of ultimate truth contained in the mythical formulations of the Church."

When I leave he takes both my hands, smiles a rare smile that reminds me of Angelo Roncalli's.

In the gardens of the society stands a sacred banyan tree, the third largest in India. This huge tree, a thousand years old, supported and splinted, is so large that five hundred people can gather under its branches. There is a sign "Silence" but the sweepers clearing fallen leaves away are singing. Men and women stand gaping at the tree. They all have shaven heads.

"Are they monks and nuns?" I ask.

"No, they are pilgrims, village people," one of the gardeners explains. "They have sacrificed their hair to a god, Sah. The priests sell it for wigs. Very profitable, Sah!"

Professor M. T. P. Mahadevan is the Director of the Center of Advanced Philosophy of the University of Madras. His hollow study on the second floor of the pink university building is a chaos of open books and papers that tremble in the sea breeze that blows into the room from the marina it overlooks. "The Advaita-Vedanta experience is identical with the Zen experience," says the slight grey-haired man behind the piled-up desk. "I often discussed this with Suzuki when we met at conferences and he agreed that Advaita is Zen, Zen is Advaita."

"Do you see Daisetz Suzuki as an important teacher?"

"He was a real guru to innumerable people! He opened many people in the West to a crucial experience of what really matters, as did my own teacher, Ramana Maharshi, 'Ramana the Great Seer.' He is very much less known in Europe and America, for he hardly wrote anything but his *Forty Verses on Existence (Ulladu Narpadu)*, the most concise, precise statement of Vedanta in modern times."

"As a student of Ramana Maharshi, would you tell me about him?"

"He was born in 1879 in Tiruculli, a village in south India, as a normal, healthy boy. At the age of seventeen he had his crucial experience; he suddenly felt gripped by the fear of impending death. He said to himself, 'Now death has come. What does it mean to die?' He felt his body die, becoming inert, and at the same time had the realization that it was not the 'I' that had died. This 'I' he experienced as something very real, the only real thing, something transcending death. His ego was lost in the flood of this self-awareness. A change in all his attitudes followed. He left home, became a *sanyassin* and lived as a hermit on a hill in Tiruvannamai, where he later built an ashram. People flocked to him in ever greater numbers, attracted by something

extraordinary that radiated from him and that I, too experienced
often. He spoke very little, but in his presence you felt time coming to a stop and experienced a stillness and peace beyond
description. He never moved out of his village. When the malignant tumor that was to kill him was diagnosed, he refused
surgery. Unconcerned, he sat like a spectator watching the disease waste his body and consoled us who grieved over him. He
died smiling, in bliss, in 1950. All he left in writing are those *Forty
Verses on Existence.* Ramana Maharshi designated the real as 'the
heart.' What he calls 'the heart,' however, is emptied of all empirical experience. The triad of fear, plurality, and ignorance—*avidya,*
or erroneous knowledge—makes for bondage. Fearlessness arises
when the nondual, true Self is realized through transcendental
insight. The so-called individual imagines that he lives in a plu-
ralistic universe, he identifies himself with his particular body,
his psychosomatic organism, and hence he expects danger from
every quarter, especially from time, otherwise called death. The
termination of this identification is *moksa,* or liberation.

"Ramana said, 'All systems of thought postulate three principles: the world, the soul, and God. These only remain three-fold
as long as egoism lasts. After this has been overcome the distinctions cease for they are the One, Brahman or Atman. But even to
say this is merely inadequate verbalization, for reality can only
be realized. If I say that the world is Brahman, it is ridiculous
because the world of our experience is impermanent, mostly
unintelligent, and full of misery. If I say that the world is non-
Brahman I also talk nonsense because there is nothing other than
Brahman. Ultimate truth is not to be attained by dialectics, but
by direct experience.

"The main purpose of the scriptures, according to Ramana, is to
expose the illusory world as such and reveal the unique Supreme
Spirit as the only reality. Hence he tells us to let the world be for
the time being and to understand the self first, to inquire into its
nature. The path prescribed by him is the inquiry 'Who am I?'
pushed to its furthest limits. Our entire psychosomatic organism,
this body with which we identify, which we speak of as 'I'

includes the very cause of our embodiment: *avidya*, which is nescience, pseudoknowledge or ignorance. If this 'ego' goes, the Self remains. It is the reality underlying the I, thou, and it. When we eradicate the ego-process to its very roots it gets resolved in the self, the many are resolved in the one.

"It is legitimate to say 'the body is I' but it is wrong to say 'the I is body.' To those who have experienced realization there is only the Self which shines forth without limit. The Self is no other than God, but God is invisible to the ego. There is no more distinction then between the seer, the seeing, and the object seen. The forms of God conceived by the ego, i.e. God seen as the Other, are images which have their relative value on the pilgrimage to ultimate truth. The very idea of release still belongs to the realm of bondage. When the ego is overcome, there is no more thought or talk about release. The means to ego-lessness is radical self-inquiry. To experience the self is Ramana's message."

"Did Ramana teach anything about interpersonal, transpersonal relationships? About social reform?"

"True transpersonal relationship is an illusion so long as the pseudo-ego is in charge. There is only transpersonal exploitation. Whenever someone came to the Maharshi to ask him what solution he had for the human miseries of poverty, illiteracy, disease, war, his advice to the social reformer took the form of a counter question, 'Have you reformed yourself first?' He used to say that, all too often, social service is mere ego-gratification, egoism that unwittingly passes itself off as altruism. Only service based on the discounting of ego can be the harbinger of good. And the egoism cannot be lessened unless one knows *existentially* that the ego is not the self and that it is this pseudo-self which is responsible for all the evil and misery in the world. And so unless one knows the true self, one cannot render adequate service to society. Self-knowledge is the knowledge that sets one free. Both the questions and the answers are necessarily in the realm of *avidya*. At best they serve as signposts towards truth and its region of silence."

"Do you feel that your contact with Ramana changed your own life and destiny?"

"To meet a sage, as I did at eighteen, is not an ordinary occurrence. To know Ramana is to be Ramana. To be Ramana is to have a full experience of nonduality. The critics of Advaita like to say that the *advaitin* is an austere intellectual, whose wells of emotion have dried up. It is an unfounded criticism, as anyone who met Ramana can testify. He was brimming with unimaginable kindness and warmth for people and animals. He never spoke of an animal as 'it,' always as 'he' or 'she'. He taught an ageless truth anew, which skeptics and agnostics as well as theists or atheists can follow in order to attain what is real. He was the supreme artist of life.

"The thought of Ramana Maharshi is indeed a perfect interpretation of Vedanta or Advaita *(ad-vaita* means without a second), the nondualism in the spirit of Shankara (ninth century). Advaita has a function to fulfill in the West, where there is nothing equivalent to it, no view that rises above the relative and relational. I am often asked if Advaita is a nondualism. I answer that the prefix *non* applies not only to duality, but to *ism* as well. For it is not a theory or philosophy, but a total existential experience, which transcends logic but is not opposed to it. Neither does it demand abdication from discursive reason or its replacement by faith. But it does not place all its trust in discursive reason alone. It is wrong to say that it is atheistic; it encompasses theistic approaches. Shankara himself wrote moving devotional poetry."

Under the desklamp a minuscule transparent fly lies on its back on my paper on the letter "I," its tiny legs folded in the prayer of rigor mortis. A large mosquito rocks back and forth on the words "Bombay, pop. 5 million," in hopeless, frenzied disorientation. It alights once more, zooms in uncoordinated circles against the bulb, crashes in the ashtray, takes a few vacillating steps in reverse, sagging through its knees, then gallantly lifts itself for the final endeavor. The large blond fly with its metallic green mask at last lies on its side, its limbs move frantically and make it turn clockwise and counterclockwise like a speedboat run aground with the outboard running wild. Its persistence is extraordinarily heroic. With singed wings it has flown at least ten sorties, crashing each time with a loud thump on its back, struggling up once more, taking off towards the irresistible Friend, the mortal Enemy. Now it lies still, only one slow front leg still defying death. Life was not flown in vain. On the green book-jacket on the periphery of the light circle, a battalion of black kamikazes, tiny as pinheads, after incredible acts of valor, rest singed and broken in the myriad postures of death.

I travel on to Bombay as if India could not be observed—minus the crumbling architecture and statuary—on one's desk. Pilgrimage to Now/Here.

Around the Jehangir Art Gallery, the sidewalk exhales human urine evaporating in the sunshine. Is this where the destitute huddle during the nights? A tall man with a shaven head, his eyes gouged out, abruptly raises two amputated arm stumps under my nose. A castrated beggar demonstrates his deficiency with an obscene grin. At the Gateway to India—the huge triumphal arch, erected in commemoration of the landing of George V and Queen Mary—a legless ten-year-old, his monstrous torso moving on its hands with grasshopper leaps, has spotted me. He vaults towards me through the traffic as a ghastly threat. I flee back across the street, irrationally impelled to avoid this confrontation at any cost. On the opposite sidewalk the torso is already waiting for me with a triumphant grimace. India wins.

In the Taj Mahal Hotel, the Victorian balconied, turreted luxury hotel, florid German and American couples loiter in the lobby shops, fondle bargains: rhinestone-trimmed trousers, raw-silk jackets for "half what you'd pay at home, *bei uns.*" The Muzak tinkles reassuringly a la Howard Johnson. In the side street around the corner from the Taj Mahal Hotel, near the main shopping street, some thirty young Swedes, Americans, Dutch lie

Rock temple Mahabalipuram
near Madras.

staring on the dirty pavement in front of a dilapidated boarding-house. Two of them strum guitars. A blue-eyed girl in greasy jeans, her Indian blouse open on pink breasts, nestles against an albino with a beard like matted angelhair. Indians stop and gape in disbelief at this foreign legion of the declining West.

Suriah Mukerjee, Ph.D., a handsome woman of forty in an elegant purple sari, has taught sociology in an American university as a Fulbright exchange professor. She also taught as a visiting professor at the University of Berlin. Now acting dean of a Bombay college, she calls herself "a progressive Brahmin," is a strict vegetarian, who neither smokes nor drinks.

"The Indian masses," she says, "don't understand anything about politics. Absolutely nothing. Our whole democratic structure is a sham, imported and superimposed. Nehru's Western ideas have never penetrated. These hippies around the corner? They may be a sign of regeneration. Unless and until you reach the level of deepest decadence and degradation, regeneration is unthinkable. That is the lesson of India. Americans? They live in the delusion that they always must do things, act constantly, manipulate God and the world, and believe that there is a solution for every problem! Americans are childish. They lack discriminating thought. There is no place for sentiment, for emotions."

I interject, "How can a sociologist repeat these worn cliches? Haven't you noticed the tortured self-questioning of America?"

"I did," she replied, "but it remains always analytical, cerebral, and conformist. There is no individual experience, no individual realization, no liberation from social molds by individual efforts, whether in the establishment or the so-called counterculture."

"In calling yourself 'a progressive Brahmin,' do you mean you are a religious Hindu?"

"Hinduism as a religion is dead; as a way of life it is very much alive. The basic ideas of Hinduism have become part of the thought and behavior patterns of our people. Don't forget

that there has never been a Hindu church, no ecclesiastical orga-
nization, no structure or administration. Our people have
prayed, built temples wherever and however they liked. The
genius of Hinduism has been through the ages to see and assert
the essential unity in the midst of the manifold expressions of
religious perceptions and formulations. Hinduism is not bothered in the least by its infinite variety of theisms, nontheisms,
polytheisms, or pantheisms. We recognize the necessity of psychological differentiation according to temperament and the
accidents of time, place, history, and education, a differentiation
which does not damage the essential unity at all. It does not
affect the much more important subjective unification of mind
and heart. Our moral code for daily life is hardly affected by our
diversity in metaphysics."

"How would you summarize the value system underlying
what you call 'Hinduism as a way of life'?"

"As I said, the metaphysical reality found through intuition and
introspection in ancient India is no longer satisfying contemporary Hindus, but the patterns of behavior and of thought that followed from these intuitions have penetrated the Indian mind and
survive. One of these is the belief in the existence of a Supreme
Being at once immanent and transcendent in the universe, an
unborn, eternal, universal Spirit, guarantee and justification of the
moral character of the universe. This Supreme Being is conceived
of as Nirguna (the attributeless God) as well as Saguna (God with
attributes) and is worshipped in the infinity of his attributes of
power, love, and perfect wisdom. Any symbol worshipped—
whether it is a stone, a tree, a mythological figure—represents the
Indescribable, the Incomprehensible, the Ineffable. Hinduism
accepts the fact that there can be no adequate likeness or image of
God, but that nevertheless men need symbols of the divine.
Brahman the Creator, Vishnu the Sustainer, and Shiva the
Destroyer symbolize some of its main distinguishable functions.
The Hindu also believes that from time to time avatars, human
manifestations of the divine occur. Rama, Krishna, Buddha, and
Jesus are among these. It is the love of God that helps man to rise

to his vocation of becoming divine and that causes the appearance of these avatars. There is an ingrained faith our people share, that the universe is a moral structure, a world of divine, spiritual immanence flowing from Shakti, the power of God. There is an ethical law, Dharma, operating in the cosmos.

"Another shared belief is in the law of karma or action. Good action brings good results; bad action results in disaster. It has nothing to do with predestination. We are determined by past action, but we are free to influence our future. So we are both free and not free! Our personal responsibility for our acts is not determined by moral conscience or by society's rules but by this built-in mechanism, this inexorable law. And closely connected with this law of karma is the belief in reincarnation, in a multitude of successive lives, needed to reach deification, instead of a single earthly life followed by a final judgment. Full acceptance of past karma, of this universal law that pervades the whole universe, is *moksa*, liberation."

"How does the karma concept affect social service and reform?"

"This is indeed a problem in modern India. Since it is generally assumed that whatever your present condition, it is the fruit of what you did before, so how could I possibly help you? The creation of social welfare and social services is constantly at loggerheads with this ingrained belief. But as secularization develops more and more, the underprivileged masses exert the necessary pressures. Of course they are resisted. One example of this pressure is the Neo-Buddhist movement started by Dr. Ambedkar, who died in the late fifties. It was actually a pseudo-religious movement, one of the attempts to break through the caste system. The idea is clever enough! Buddha had condemned the caste system 2,500 years ago; Hinduism in its petrified state is still clinging to it. In Ambedkar's vision Neo-Buddhism would restore the human dignity of the Untouchables. It is emphatically social and secular in tendency and in reality it has become a political movement with a religious label."

"Do you see the eventual disappearance of the caste system?"

"It will take a long time. It is too ingrained. Twenty years ago, when I married a man belonging to a sub-caste only slightly below mine, both our families disowned us for years. Caste can't be wished away."

The 707 to Delhi is overloaded. "Indian Airlines," sneers my neighbor, "is having its jets outfitted with running boards, so it can take a few extra passengers. Safety? Who cares? It is money that matters." The big plane lifts itself laboriously and circles over Bombay.

"Look," points my neighbor, "there are the Towers of Silence."

All I see is a spot where dense flocks of birds are circling.

"These are the vultures," he sneers again, "that pick the bones of us devout Parsis when our bodies are exposed on the Towers, according to age-old custom, lest the sacred earth be contaminated by our rotting human flesh."

To see or not to see Agra is the question. But to cross India and to miss the Taj Mahal, is all too mortal a sin, all too evil an omen. An after-image of Agra is a sprawling slum of forty thousand, where all that is lame, stunted, predatory, sick, starved in the world seems to grovel below the stone heap that once was the great Red Fort. From this burrow of wretchedness rise the imperial conceits: Itmad-ud-Daula, a royal tomb of latticed, fluted, white marble that looks like a music box, and the Taj Mahal which, to my ingrate eye—instantly allergic to islands of Moghul grandeur in oceans of destitution—is an esthete's conspicuous confection, with its dome as large as St. Peter's, molded in immaculately refined sugar. Where kitsch stops, art may start.

Akbar, that remarkable emperor who made Agra his capital, first built the Red Fort as his residence, then constructed Fatehpur Sikri as an even more overwhelmingly magnificent residence. For sixteen short years, surrounded by his eight hundred concubines and thousands of elephants—as if one concubine and a dozen elephants wouldn't suffice—he lived there. He sat on his throne atop the octagonal pillar in the splendid hall and enjoyed the disputations of the Hindu, Muslim, Buddhist, and Christian theologians he invited, until Fatehpur Sikri ran out of water and had to be abandoned. In its heyday it was, as an English traveler wrote in 1574, "greater than London."

Three years before his death Akbar started to construct his last residence, his mausoleum at Sikandra, after having chiseled on Fatehpur Sikri's lofty gate, "The world is but for an hour, spend it in devotion, the rest is unseen."

Guarded by a massive gateway of red sandstone inlaid with marble, flanked by the inevitable minarets, Akbar's grave is reached through a dank, sloping tunnel. Almost imperceptibly a wisp of light filters through a small aperture near the high ceiling to make the crypt into a cube of transparent shadow with, at its center, a raised slab of stone covered by a black shroud. On it visitors have left a few faded yellow flowers. A copper lantern swings dead above the emperor's grave. Itmad-ud-Daula and the Taj speak neither of life nor of death, only of "Me," of hubris perpetuated. Akbar's grave is a pilgrim's "must."

Once more outside. The gardens of Sikandra spring abruptly, ardently to life in the setting sun. Tiny chipmunks shoot up the trunks of the mimosa trees, flights of grass-green parrots with long tails flap their short stubby wings, dozens of pearly grey doves sit on the stone benches, little red-faced monkeys flee in comic fright as a family of black-faced langur monkeys, tall as German shepherds, clamber down a stone wall for sunset frolics. Two boys with sticks try to chase them back. To the langurs it is all part of the evening entertainment. In huge, courtly leaps, tails elegantly curved, they float across the lawns in large circular patterns, the young clinging to their mothers' bellies.

The last after-image is of emaciated sacred cows, their calves nuzzling flabby udders, probing piles of stinking rubbish for something edible. In the eyes of two mangy camels blocking traffic near the Taj, distilled contempt for all that is human, glances of bottomless disillusionment, of unconditional insubordination. *Kyrie Eleison.*

Akbar's grave

New Year's Offerings, MacLeod Ganj.

⚵ *Dharamsala* ⚵

The train crawls to Delhi through endless plains of yellow dust. Here and there a clump of trees, a ruined temple, a cluster of huts, a defunct brick house. In the ochre fields everywhere people are squatting, defecating. Wherever one looks out of a train window in India, there are these isolated humans squatting. Continent of incontinence.

In London just before the war, I befriended a Hindu philosopher, a pockmarked wiry little fireball of a Hindu, much older than I, who was writing his thesis at the School of Oriental Studies. Then he returned to his lectureship at the University of Delhi, war broke out, and we lost contact. Leafing through the telephone book I find a listing for a Prof. Sri Krishna Saxena. He recognizes my voice instantly. "I have so often thought of you," he crows in his Indian waterfall-English. "And I live around the corner from your hotel."

"Come and have breakfast with us tomorrow morning, Sri Krishna!"

"Splendid, splendid!" he yells back.

At eight-thirty, I watch a heavy-set old man in grey Nehru jacket and white lunghi, supporting himself on a cane, cross the lobby to the reception desk. I study the fleshy face, try to reconstruct the Sri Krishna I once knew. I only recognize pockmarks. Then I see my own face in the large, gilded mirror opposite me, see it through Sri Krishna's eyes.

"I retired to New Delhi only a few years ago, as Emeritus Professor of the University of Hawaii and do I hate to be emeritus!" Sri Krishna says. "Do I hate it! Can't you find me a job in the States? I am only sixty-eight."

"Grow a beard, Sri Krishna, a long white beard. Call yourself Swami Sri Krishna and try our free enterprise system. Swamis are still booming in the States, both in the flesh and on TV."

"The pity of it is that I don't believe anymore in all our

Oriental claptrap," he says while picking his teeth and belching in the finest Oriental tradition.

"Have you written a lot since London?"

"Only what is necessary for a professor. Four books, some forty articles, and lots of book reviews on Indian philosophy, of course. There is no more depressing job than exposing all the bloody nonsense foreigners write about our philosophies and religions. Both Hindus and Buddhists have almost given up being bothered! Of course an excellent work appears once in a while. What nauseates me is when Christians who ought to know better, as for instance that Oxford professor, who dares to write as if all mankind had been bereft of God until he revealed himself in the person of Jesus Christ. As if all religion before that were an antipasto for the Last Supper!

"The word *revelation* to us is experiential. Revelatory knowledge is not 'spoken' by God, but intuitively perceived by us! Nor do we use *incarnation* in the Christian sense. A Gandhi may in the future be regarded as a divine incarnation. We also regard Jesus as an incarnation of God, but not the only one. Our seekers discovered the mysteries of the inner life in a way analogous to that in which today we discover empirically the mysteries of the physical universe; there is no "revealed" cosmology, geography, and physics, is there?

"Well, Hinduism and Buddhism made certain discoveries about the nature of being human and about the universe, and these discoveries determine our attitude towards prayer, meditation, and worship. To look at all this from the point of view of a Christian dogmatic and revelatory standpoint is silly and irrelevant. Now, as far as God is concerned, either he revealed himself to us before Christ or he didn't. If he didn't, we deserve some credit for having discovered him all on our own. We just couldn't wait! We are not a godless people. Indian preoccupation with that very divine life is often blamed for our material backwardness! In India God has survived neglect and denial by Jains, Buddhists, Advaitins, and that without revealing himself to some chosen bunch at a specific date in a specific place. It was just all too odd of God—in view of the available communication facilities at the time—to have selected Jerusalem and the Jews. Anyhow, God must have muddled his revelation quite poorly, for it seems to be in need of constant 'authoritative interpretation' by popes and synods, whose interpretation then determines the content and meaning of the revelation. Just the other day the ex-Holy Office warned again that it is not the dead letter of scripture that is definitive, but the living magisterium of the Church. Now please find me a job as a non-Swami."

"What is the elixir of wisdom you propose to bring to the West?"

"That the Christianity of the Sermon on the Mount is as good as any, so long as it is not treated as if it were an ethic for merchants. For it is the ethic of enlightenment. No Oriental claptrap is needed. I am a modern man. I even admire you Americans' excursions to the moon, although I can't help wondering how these astronauts will die. Has the quality of life and death changed since the Vedas, even in space, in a space module? If we Hindus have just one merit, it is that at any rate we have thought for a few millennia about life, pain, old age, death. We discovered that there is a soul, an Atman, which is not the same as the ego, so that it is not the 'I' that gets old, suffers from toothache and cancer. The discovery has even been known to work! We may not have been shooting at the moon, but we have thought of the real problems. Maybe you Americans will get around to thinking seriously about the real problems during your moon vacations."

Behind the hotel, on Ring Road, a monastery-like building with Buddhist banners intrigued me. At the far end of a green courtyard the doors of a temple stood wide open. On the grass, Mongolian-looking women were playing with their children in the morning sun. The temple, modern and light, was dominated by a single large Buddha in meditation. No one spoke enough English to answer my questions, but the taxi driver set out looking for an interpreter. At long last a reserved Indian woman in a dark blue sari appeared.

the Red Fort of Delhi

"This is a colony for Tibetan refugees," she explained. "What you see around the courtyard are their one-room apartments. I am the doctor here. Are you European tourists?"

"We were both born in Holland, but are American citizens," I explained, "and I happen to be a doctor too, or rather I was one for a while."

She dropped her disguise of reserve, became friendly, and invited us into her bare consulting room to talk shop.

"I love these Tibetans. They are strong and enormously good-humored people. I became interested in Tibetans because of the connection between heart-pathology—I am a cardiologist—and their adaptation to altitude. Interestingly, these people have a high incidence of heart disease when they are at low altitudes! There is a lot of tuberculosis too. Of course there is also a lot of arthritis; these people carry enormous loads all their lives. We have another refugee camp on the other side of the river. Some two thousand Tibetans live there in tents."

Dr. Sneh Gadhoke's movements had the acquired angularity of a feminine woman doing a man's job.

"You mention hygiene," I said, "I can't imagine how children can survive at all in the poor sections of the Indian cities I have seen."

"We develop fantastic immunities," she said. "Europeans who get dysentery here become deadly ill. Millions of Indians have these chronic gastrointestinal infections, but are hardly bothered by them. This morning I saw two little boys sitting on the sidewalk. One dropped his *chappati* in the gutter, fished it out and ate it with gusto! Of course they have all kinds of worms, but they seem to live in some kind of symbiosis with them. Once a child has escaped lethal infections until the age of five, it has a good chance of surviving to a respectable age. Proteins? They are probably less important, especially after early youth, than is assumed. The main source of protein in the Indian vegetarian diet is *dhal*, made of lentils or dried peas. I think frankly that our people are so strong, survive so miraculously, simply because they eat little and few of them have sedentary occupations. Talking about food, why don't you have lunch with us?"

The taxi headed for the Tibetan camp, a village of hundreds of canvas tents and straw lean-tos, all flying long banners of orange, sky blue, milky pink, green with white squares, yellow with red stripes, transparent viridian. A few dozen Tibetans surrounded the taxi. The faces of moon-faced children and wrinkled old women were all smiling. The taxi driver Channan Singh, a middle-aged Sikh with extraordinarily fine eyes, translated patiently, very kindly, enjoying it, his eyes all soul.

"There are two thousand of us here. We knit sweaters and handbags. We make tents and tarpaulins. We deliver them to Tibet House, which sells them all the way to America. Are you from America? Yes? Where are you going from Delhi?"

"Tomorrow," I said, "we are going to Dharamsala, to visit His Holiness."

"What? You know His Holiness?"

The smiles became ecstatic; they couldn't believe it.

"It is true," I said. "I am very interested in Buddhism. I am going to speak with the Dalai Lama. I shall give him your regards."

"Tell him '*Tashi Delé*,' 'Happy New Year' from us! Next week is Tibetan New Year, that's why we have all the flags out."

"I shall wish His Holiness '*Tashi Delé*' from you. May I leave something to buy sweets for the children?"

An old woman received the money in both hands, folded her hands before her chest and bowed. The money was not received as alms, but as a gift.

"What else do you do apart from weaving handbags and knitting sweaters?"

"Our men build roads."

"Aren't you cold in these tents?"

"We are used to that. We'd rather be cold than hot. That's why we don't stay here during the summer. We leave for the hill country in March. The food is cheaper here, but it is too hot for us. So every spring we have a procession and then we leave for Simla with everything we have, our tents and flags, and even our lamas."

Tibetan refugee encampment

"Tashi Delé! Tashi Delé! Tashi Delé!"

A few hundred yards from the camp, on the banks of the Yamuna River stands a lonely square temple.

"Is this a Sikh temple?"

"Yes indeed," says Channan Singh, "one of our oldest. Foreigners never see it, for they never come to this side of the river.

The square terrace on the Yamuna is empty. He insists on showing off the interior of the temple, characteristically bare in its Sikh austerity, and fetches the temple priest, Sewadar Gurbusc Singh, a kindly man of seventy, straight as a cedar, dignified as a king, and probably poor as a mouse. I start to draw the temple to please Channan Singh, who is so obviously proud of it. The priest stands immobile, noticing that I am drawing him too. Channan Singh squats on the ground and translates the old man's story:

"Here a Muslim fakir once lived a lonely life of prayer, fasting, and penitence. His vigils and fasts made him so thin and his yearning for Allah made him so mad that people called him Majnu. He was visited by the Sikh prophet Guru Nanak, the founder of our Sikh religion. Under Nanak he promptly reached full enlightenment and became a devout disciple of the guru. This hermitage on this small hillock on the banks of the Yamuna is still known as Gurudawara Majnu Tila.

"There are other legends connected with this place, Sah. Nanak raised one of Emperor Ibrahim Lodi's favorite elephants from the dead on this spot and Guru Hargobind, when he was invited by Emperor Jehangir, also stayed here. But the emperor got suspicious and imprisoned him in Gwalor Fort. He was going to be released, but prevailed on Jehangir to free all his 52 fellow prisoners. It is a very holy place, Gurudawara Majnu Tila."

There is a curious peacefulness about the bare imageless temple. The foliage of the trees seems cooler and lacier, our voices sound deeper, all normal background noises have disappeared.

The air, the voices, the trees, the light ochre walls have a transparency as of muslin, the sun is strong but throws no shadows.

"What does 'Gurudawara' mean?" I ask Singh in the taxi. We have become friends, feel an affectionate respect for one another, a kind of love that comes from nothing but observing the other man's eyes seeing. There is no mistaking it.

"It means," said Singh, "it means . . . well I am sorry, Sah, I am not sure. You said you are leaving tomorrow for Dharamsala? At what time? I'll find it out for you."

Next morning at the Old Delhi station Singh is waiting with a slip of paper. On it is written: "Gurudawara means 'Door of God' or 'Place where God lives.'"

Channan Singh—a place where God lives.

The compartment windows and doors of the train have double locks which one is pointedly advised to secure carefully before going to sleep. We huddle in overcoats, put on three pairs of socks against the biting cold. The night is endless. At dawn the train comes to a stop for the hundredth time. It has been crawling slower and slower for the last hour. This stop is unusually long. Passengers on the platform of the tiny station wrapped in blankets, jump about to get warm. The stationmaster with turned-up waxed mustache is arguing with the figures in blankets. The station sentry, a dull, middle-aged soldier in threadbare khaki with an antique rifle slung over his shoulder, is surrounded by another vehement group. No one speaks a word of English. The teen-age son of the lady in the compartment next door brings us tea from a thermos bottle with the compliments of his mother, the radiantly charming wife of the brigadier general in command of Srinagar.

"Why are we stuck here?"

"Someone forgot to put water in the engine at the last station, so we ran out of steam," she explains. "It may take another three or four hours."

Outside, the endless plain lies under morning mist, vaguely yellow green. A tree in the middle distance seems heavy with what look like huge black pears. Suddenly I see they are vultures. They

stretch their naked necks, alight, circle on lazy wings. Then they sit
down on their tree, pull in their necks, become pears again. On the
far right a camel shuffles its eternal round at a waterwell.

We arrive in Pathankot six hours late.

The bus for Dharamsala is a hybrid, Dodge with Mercedes grill,
wooden benches, no shock absorbers, and a steering wheel that
shrieks ominously in falsetto. We, the lucky ones, sit six abreast,
luggage piled in our laps, as in a 707 in extreme turbulence. The
standing ones hold on to one another. The driver, an old, thin
Mongolian type, passes trucks and lazy buses on the craggy left
shoulder of a narrow tree-lined road that reminds me of one in
Provence. Tiny villages of chalet-like trellised cottages fly by. In
a yellow alfalfa field forty vultures contest a scarlet carcass with
a white dog. Slowly the road rises into the Himalayan foothills.
After two hours the green landscape becomes burnt sienna, the
bus storms along ravines of red clay and moraines strewn with
gigantic boulders. It crosses torrents, rapid rivulets, and dry
riverbeds. While passing cars, buses, and herds, the driver's face
remains impassively Mongolian, but the long yellow teeth clatter
and the lips are in constant motion, swearing or praying.

The man next to me feeds bananas to the boy in his lap and
offers me a piece as prelude to conversation. He is a doctor from
Rishikesh.

"What country are you from? Is that your wife? How many
children have you? How long have you been married?"

"Fifteen years," I confess. Indians ask anything; it is up to you
to answer or not.

"How old is your son?"

"Seventeen. "

"How could that be?"

"Well, he is from my first marriage."

"Ah, divorce. It is too easy in the West. In India it is very, very
difficult, fortunately. We frown upon it," he crows above the
noise of the bus, "frown, frown! Take my sister! Her husband
was no good, he ran away! For eight years they were separated!

But my sister remained faithful to him! You see, Indian boys and girls are virgins when they marry! If a girl has loved a boy and she must marry another, she forgets the first one, never thinks of him again, never, for she respects her husband! We are a chaste people, not like people in the West! My sister remained faithful. Now, her husband's parents have convinced him that he was bad to her. Now he knows what is good and what is bad, you see, so now they are together again and I am taking their boy back to them. They are very happy now! She waited and waited till he called for her! Divorce is no good, freedom leads to badness."

I nod, giddy, his finger shakes too close to my eye.

The bus careens through appalling curves, the guardrails are broken or absent. Deep below lie green valleys. The Himalayas now are on top of us. We rush through villages, where girls don't wear saris but trousers or long dirty skirts in sweetish colors and silver or gold nose ornaments that stretch all the way from nose to ear, covering half their faces with intricate metal tumors. Men are dressed in long white tunics of rough wool, their belts are coils of black rope.

"Do you read Vedanta, the Upanishads?" I ask him.

He gives me an astonished look. "That's what we have Brahmins for! I am a doctor!"

He wants to talk shop. I ask him about hepatitis.

"Hepatitis? Very frequent indeed. It is endemic! Mostly it comes from onions, especially raw onions! Yes!"

"Do you give gamma globulin?"

He looks nonplussed. "No," he exclaims then, with that scientifically-ignorant look that should be called "doctors'-stare," "no, I give milk, condensed milk. Much better than tea. Coffee is very bad! Indian coffee is bad. Onions are very bad!"

I feign enthusiastic assent.

"How about venereal disease, Doctor?" He swallows his banana.

"Terrible," he shouts, "atrocious! Especially in congested areas! Especially syphilis! It is getting difficult to treat! Penicillin used to work like magic but no more, no more! Gonorrhea too is terribly resistant. Very vexing for the doctor! They always blame us doctors!"

"How do you account for the rapid spread of gonorrhea and syphilis with all the chastity?"

"Ah," he says excitedly, "industrialization is to blame! In the big cities the men are absent, they work far from home. The ladies are alone all day and they may become sexually desirous and then give their bodies to a man! And then, excuse me, in subsequent sexual acts they may infect their husbands. Very vexing for us physicians!"

He leans across me, jerks the window down, and vomits.

"Excuse me," he says, "it is the bananas."

It has become mercifully dark; the bus still skids through hairpin-turns, but the abysses disappear as if by magic. We arrive at Dharamsala eight hours behind schedule.

"Dharamsala," says the folder, "is the headquarters of the Kangra district of Himachal Pradesh, a delightful hill station, reached by rapid comfortable buses from Pathankot. It is closer to the Himalaya snowline than any other hill station. The climate is bracing. There is a choice of excellent hotels, a government rest house, a tourist bungalow. It is the seat of the Dalai Lama."

My visit to the Dalai Lama was not planned. At the time of my pilgrimage, His Holiness was not yet the public figure he has become in recent years. I was booking my trip to Sri Lanka, India, and Japan when the travel agent, a rotund little man with a wreath of white whisps around a gleaming bald pate asked, "Wouldn't you like to visit the Dalai Lama?"

"Of course," I said, "but how does one go about that?"

"Very simple!" he smiled. "I'll arrange it for you. I know all the Tibetans at the U.N. I take care of all their trips."

I could have kissed the gleaming pate. . .

I had counted on exploring those excellent hotels at leisure in the early afternoon, but it is now nine and pitch-dark.

"The Tourist Hotel"—a dirty yellow cube—"very posh, very clean, good food," the doctor in the bus has assured me, stands close to the bus stop. Under a bare bulb, a faded sign reads: "Modern rooms. Private baths. Oriental and Western cuisine."

The dark taproom smells of sweat. On half of the tables lamps with tiny bulbs create atmosphere. The phonograph sounds like an asthmatic seal. A couple of forlorn lovers hold hands in the gloom. The elderly owner in shirtsleeves and citron-yellow turban, bows like the maitre d'hotel at Maxim's. We sit down on a rickety bench in one of the booths, drink tea from dirty cups .

There is a telephone. I call the Government Rest House, no answer, the Tourist Bungalow, no vacancy. With another elegant bow, the owner presents a greasy menu.

"Our staff is on vacation," he says, "but I could make you parathas. I also have some cold mutton on toast."

He puts the guestbook in front of me on the grimy table. I glance at my predecessor in misfortune, and read: Beethoven, Ludwig van, mechanic, U.S.A., date of arrival 12/5/1978, date of departure 8/9/1840. Address: YU 8-7432.

"Is this correct?" I ask, showing him my entry.

"Sorry, Sah, I can't read."

Our room has wooden bedsteads, covered with eiderdowns black with years of grime. Underneath the comforters there is no mattress. A wooden bottom of planks is stamped "This side up."

"Is there no bedding?"

"Guests usually bring their own, Sah. I think I have two sheets, but they cost extra.

"And towels, please!" He returns with a tiny pink towel decorated with the word *Hers*.

The climate is bracing, around 15 degrees. We sit on a newspaper spread over the comforters and read the Hsin-hsin Ming, "There is no here, no there. Infinity is before our eyes. The infinitely large is as small as the infinitely minute. If one wishes to turn to the One Vehicle, one must have no aversion to the objects of the senses.

At dawn through the window, across a dull green valley the white snow cliffs of Dhaudalar rise up as a perpendicular wall. The little bus up the final 2,000 feet to the Dalai Lama's village is a cable car without cable. It stops in a different world.

In the middle of the wide main street of McLeod Ganj stands a white pagoda. Women in heavy dark woolen skirts with multicolored striped aprons, men in black baggy Tibetan coats and high embroidered boots of red felt circumambulate the shrine, turn the prayer wheels, two-foot-high drums of polished brass. A little market ablaze with the colors of fresh fruit and vegetables is crowded with Tibetans. Their wide, high-cheekboned faces are serene, ready to break into smiles on any pretext. I buy biscuits for our breakfast in a dilapidated general store. The owners, Parsis who speak English, look like Jewish shopkeepers in a Kansas prairie town.

It is a fifteen-minute climb from the village to the Dalai Lama's compound. Old Tibetan women, bent under loads of firewood, fold their hands in greeting, children hold their hands together in front of their chest, smile and bow. Patriarchal old men in fur caps with earflaps, turning a prayer wheel, immersed in prayer, pass me chanting. Over the great valley, large white birds circle in clear, thin air. At the gate of the compound armed Indian guards check passports, telephone the Dalai Lama's secretary, Lama Tenzing Geiche, who has been expecting us since yesterday. In the drawing room, where holy books wrapped in orange and blue cloth fill the shelves of glassed bookcases, we talk about Sri Lanka and Hinayana Buddhism, about Africa and Schweitzer.

"By the way, where are you staying?"

He knows all about the Tourist Hotel.

"We can accommodate you in the guest cottage of His Holiness, but it is a steep thirty-minute climb, do you mind? His Holiness will make time for you in a few days. We'll be in touch."

Our path leads past the barbed-wire fence that surrounds the

Tibetans at McLeod Ganj

compound. An Indian soldier, rifle at his side, stands dozing in front of his sentry box, another sentry has made a fire and is cooking lunch. The trail, part path, part rock-hewn staircase, winds along the edge of a steep precipice. From bushes and trees wave faded gauze prayer flags. Every few yards people have built stone heaps, symbolical mandalas, from two to five feet high. On a large bare rock the words OM MANI PADME HUM—"Om, the jewel in the Lotus"—have been carved in large Tibetan script, filled in with red, white, yellow, blue, and green paint. At the cottage, on the wide terrace overlooking the splendid immensity of valley, the housekeeper awaits us with her little daughter. We have a whole suite to ourselves! There is a cozy sitting room, logs are burning in the fireplace, a clean bedroom with a stone floor, a bathroom, even a water heater! A maid with a lovely flat Tibetan moon face, quietly puts tea and biscuits in front of the fire. Dawa Chodon speaks a little English.

"Please rest," she says, "you must be hungry. Lunch will be ready soon."

I take Claske by the shoulders. Was last night a dream? Is this a dream?

And I repeat the words of Shah Jahan on the Red Fort in Delhi, "If paradise be on the face of the earth, this is it, this is it, this is it!"

On the "cathedral," the main Temple, Buddhist flags are blowing. Their colors represent the "Original Nature," Lama Geshei Lobsay Luntok explains.

What is this "Original Nature," the "Self-nature?" Hui Hai in the eighth century said, "That you have not recognized it does not mean it is not there. Why? Because observation, perception, recognition is that Self-nature itself. Without it, it would be impossible to perceive anything ever." On some flags, mantras and prayers are written. Each time the flag moves in the wind, it recites the prayer.

"Is it the wind that moves? Is it the flag that moves?" the disciples ask a Zen master.

"It is your mind moving," answers the Roshi.

Inside the cathedral the silver shawms are blown, inviting the
Bodhisattva to descend, a Buddhist *Veni Creator* which is part of
the Vajrayana discipline of meditation and visualization. The
huge horns sound to underline the sayings of the Buddha.

"How many Tibetans are there in India?" I ask the Lama.

"Ninety thousand of the six million who are still in Tibet.
People go through incredible hardships to escape. Some succeed;
they are arriving all the time. No, we had no caste system like
India. That is incorrect. Not that we were a classless society, of
course. Some professions were held in low esteem: butchers, for
instance. There was an aristocracy and a laboring class, but there
was no real serfdom. If one had five or six servants and did not
get on with one or two of them, they were sometimes transferred to neighbors. Often families of servants were not paid in
money, but in land and houses, for generations. This land they
tilled in their spare time. They were members of the family in a
way. Often they inherited everything from childless couples and
then they 'jumped' class! There was no military caste; soldiers,
officers came from all walks of life, but very often they were
Khampas from eastern Tibet, who are more martial and short-
tempered than the peaceful Lhasa people. Everyone, regardless
of background, could become a lama. We have a saying, 'If
someone has intellect, nothing prevents him from sitting on the
highest religious throne.'

"The Dalai Lama and the Panchen Lama lived in perfect harmony until the Chinese in 1950 tried to create a rift. The last
Panchen Lama was appointed by the Chinese, ignoring all the
ritual procedure. There was no real conflict between the sects,
the Yellow Hats and the Red Hats, until the Chinese tried to
divide them for their own political reasons. The Dalai Lama is
both our spiritual leader and secular administrator.

"When in 1933 the thirteenth Dalai Lama felt he was going to
die, he called his ministers together who had to function until
his new reincarnation could be found, and gave them certain
instructions. After his death he was placed on a throne. The
head of the corpse was facing south, but turned towards the

east. A great star-shaped fungus appeared on a pillar pointing northeast. These were omens of where the new incarnation might be found.

"A delegation of high officials departed. They came to a sacred lake, where according to tradition visions appeared in the water. After several days of prayer and meditation they saw visions appear in the lake: the Tibetan letters Ah, Ka, and Ma, a monastery and a farmhouse. These signs were interpreted. Ah stood for Amdo, the district, Ka for the monastery Kumbum, Ma for another monastery near the village of Takster in northeastern Tibet, where the delegation eventually recognized the farmhouse. Here a boy, then barely two years old, was found and carefully tested. The child recognized the walking stick, the prayer drum, and the rosary of his predecessor and knew the names of the principal dignitaries of the search party. The fourteenth reincarnate Dalai Lama of Tibet had been discovered."

I ask, "There are those stories about lamas who can cover immense distances in seconds, who can lie down in the snow and develop such heat that the snow melts around them, et cetera. Are these just popular legends or are they true?"

"True," says the lama.

"Did anyone who could perform such feats escape from Tibet?"

The lama falls silent. Then he says, "I am not authorized to tell. These supernatural powers are not really important. Realization is important. The main purpose of meditation is not only for the present life but for future life. The lowest level of desire is to be born in the next life as a human being or as a celestial being. The middle level is to be free in the next life of all desire, greed, delusion. The highest level of desire is to be of service to all living creatures, to be a Bodhisattva."

On the steep trail we overtake an old woman turning her prayer wheel, praying in sing-song.

"The prayer wheel is not used only by the unsophisticated believer, but also by mature Tibetan Buddhists as an aid to concentration, to keep the surface mind busy," the lama had told us.

She bows and smiles with half-closed Buddha eyes. In her ears hang large turquoise earrings. Other women with huge loads of leaves and branches on their backs come scrambling up the trail alongside the abyss.

Eagles sail like huge seagulls, their white bellies shine in the sun, gold-brown heads spy left, right, right, left. Lower in the champagne air circle black crows, vultures, and hawks. Deeper still, thousands of feet below, beige birds fly in formation. On our left the sheer cliff of the Dhaudalar rises in endless vertical perspectives of snow. A shepherd with a wounded sheep on his shoulders staggers up the steep rocky steps, his legs trembling under the load. He pauses, puts the animal down. It stands there quiet and sad.

Close to the OM MANI PADME HUM rock the owner of the Tourist Hotel comes limping down the path, leaning on a cane and with a bible under his arm. His turban looks soiled. He smiles and waves his cane in greeting. Here anything can happen. The man gets closer and I realize it is the innkeeper's double. He stops, gestures broadly that he is a deaf-mute, then opens the greasy leatherbound book and shows us recommendations and testimonials. He is a great clairvoyant, according to testimonials from the principal of Pathankot High School, the stationmaster of Srinagar, a certain Lama Lobsang Dhondup, and other unimpeachable authorities. He motions us to sit down on a rock, tears a square piece of paper out of his book. We must write down our age. He signals eloquently that we have one son, he needs his age too. I must fold the paper containing these vital statistics and hold it in a closed fist. He covers his eyes with a grimy hand, turns his head away demonstratively, and opens his book. He writes down my age, that of Claske, and that of Lukas. Correct! Then he writes down the date of our flight to India after a gifted impersonation of a Boeing in flight. Our future is shaping up rather favorably. Lukas is not going into the army and will be a writer; we shall live to the ripe ages of 88

and 85 respectively. Claske will suffer aches and pains in her
arms and back (he mimes like a Marceau clown now, rubbing
the small of his back) between the ages of 65 and 70. Then she
will be in the pink of condition for her last fifteen years on earth.
He demonstrates her unimpeded bliss by standing up straight
with a beatific smile at the heavens, pulls a thick watch out of
his waistcoat to indicate he has other momentous appointments
to keep and writes our bill. His honorarium is thirty rupees. I
offer ten, which he accepts with dignity. I take his hand, stare
into it, and write down, "You are 58." He looks at me admir-
ingly, shakes yes. I write down, "You owe me five rupees." He
laughs and laughs, makes his belly tremble and shake, waves a
finger into my face, hahaha, and hurries down the mountain to
his important appointment.

In the undergrowth the three large black-faced monkeys with
white collars that sat watching the performances leap down into
the abyss.

In the early afternoon the Indian guards at the gate of the official
compound copy our passports. We are frisked, have to leave
matches, pen knife, even a nail file.

His Holiness, the fourteenth Dalai Lama, Sakya Gejong Tenzin
Gyatsho, is tall, surprisingly young, with a smile that is exceptionally radiant, even for a Tibetan. He shakes hands informally
and points at a modern Swedish settee opposite him. His room
is bright and comfortable, the furniture simple and modern.
Although his English is excellent, Tenzing Geiche helps out with
a word here and there. When a young lama comes in with coffee, I have to move over and sit next to the Dalai Lama. He
keeps replenishing my cup from a silver coffeepot. Tenzing
Geiche has obviously briefed him. He wants to hear all about
my trans-religious "Pacem in Terris" sanctuary in Warwick, N.Y.,
and what it has taught me about the spirituality of the young.

"I too have met very many young people in these last eleven
years of exile. I have come to see that cultural and age gaps are
almost always spiritual gaps. The young, the hippies? They

Lamas chanting sutras, Dharamsala.

come in dozens to Dharamsala. What does it matter that they look unkempt? They express the hopelessness of people when their traditional cultural ideals suddenly reveal themselves as being empty of meaning. Long hair does not stand in the way of the search for ultimate meaning, neither does a shaven head help it," he smiles, rubbing his own.

"Of course Buddhism must have an enormous attraction for people, when the sponginess, the hollowness of power, the unreliability of money, of status, all the doubtful benefits of 'progress' dawn upon them. It must be a revelation then to find a religion which sees the 'Jewel in the Lotus,' the Buddha-nature, not only in every human being, but even in every sentient being, a religion that gives a supreme meaning and vocation, an infinite dignity to every human life, and which puts the responsibility for attaining the supreme insight squarely on one's own shoulders and stimulates us to reach it by our own efforts. The good qualities in humanity are our only hope. This doesn't mean at all that the bad ones are overlooked or ignored, but that the basic quality that tends to be good and noble must be recognized, emphasized, cultivated, encouraged. Where else lies hope?"

He has been told of my work with Albert Schweitzer.

"I have been fascinated with Dr. Schweitzer from the time I was a little boy. Tell me, tell me."

For an hour or so I reminisce about my work with the "Grand Docteur" at the hospital at Lambaréné, but he keeps asking questions.

"What is your final evaluation of Albert Schweitzer?"

"He was one of the three men in my life who have given me most. Schweitzer was a very great human being, almost over life-size, and a pioneer. As a doctor, as early as 1913, he was a pioneer in true foreign aid to the needy, without any political or religious strings attached. As a theologian he was a pioneer in a new approach to biblical research. As a musician he was responsible for one of the few things that do honor to our time: the rediscovery of Johann Sebastian Bach. At age 86 he was still a pioneer, this time in his protest against atom-bomb testing. He was also a pioneer in missionary work, placing service above the obsession with nominal conversion. He was a pioneer in practical ecumenism. As doctor, musician, philosopher he pushed every one of his potentialities to its furthest limits. What more may one expect from a man?"

"How about his 'Reverence for Life'?"

"It was a noble inspiration. He gave me a photograph of the spot on the Ogowé River where in 1915 it came to him as a transcendental experience, an illumination. Still, to me, 'I have reverence for life' is an amazing statement. What is that 'I' that has reverence for life? As if there were a dichotomy between 'I' and 'life!' As if 'I' were anything but 'life!' One step further and he would have broken through the barrier of ego and he would be my third Bodhisattva. Now I honor his memory as that of a great man, a great personality with whom I was privileged to work, a great ego."

"You have just touched on something very crucial, on the split between 'I' and 'the other,' between 'I' and 'life itself.' In this all schools of Buddhism (as it is called in the West; we prefer the traditional term Dharma) agree. The quintessence of Dharma is that one understands the causes in oneself of one's own *dukkha*, or pain, thereby becoming able to tell others of these causes. Precisely your question 'Who is this "I" who has reverence?' is indeed solved in Buddhist thought, which says, 'To suppose that things and beings exist independently, have an ego-nature, is the atman-view and this is still ignorance. For one who is freed, this ego-view is destroyed. It is the highest aspect of insight. This does not mean that the sense objects perceived by the five senses are negated, but that our conventional, relativistic view of them is seen as being incomplete. The living person who goes on from day to day is real enough, but the innate Me-feeling of all beings has only a relative reality. One of the virtues of a Buddha is that he lets the rain of his friendliness and compassion fall steadily and continuously upon all suffering beings.'"

"I believe, Your Holiness, that what you have just expressed is the neglected essence of Christianity as well as Buddhism. A

Christian mystic, Tauler, has said, 'Nothing burns in hell but the
ego.' One could paraphrase this, 'Nothing is crucified but ego;
nothing is resurrected but Christ!'"   + Albert Schweitzer

"Who are the other two men who meant so much to you?"

"The others are Pope John and Daisetz Teitaro Suzuki. All
three were over eighty when I met them, all three had a spirit
that was eternally young. Pope John is the one I love most, for
he was all warmth and humanness. I see him as a genius of the
heart, as a Catholic Bodhisattva, who far transcended being a
pope. In his last years I believe he was truly enlightened, his ego
had dissolved. Not a trace of narcissism was left. Whatever he
did came from the self. 'I am only the pope,' he would say. He
had overcome all prejudices. He had overcome the theology of
the scribes, which has estranged us from the Light that enlight-
ens every individual who comes into the world. Having overcome his own ego, the Church as collective ego did not worry
him very much. Speaking of his own impending death he said:
'My bags are packed.' His humor, his tolerance, freedom, compassion, his wisdom, his intrepidity, all were integrated. To me
he was proof that enlightenment can be reached through any
spiritual discipline, in his case a very conventional Catholic one.
To put it in Christian terms I see him as a manifestation of the
Holy Spirit."

The Dalai Lama smiled his assent and asked, "And Suzuki?"

"I came upon his writings about thirty years ago as upon a revelation, and he has remained my almost daily companion. He is
one of those rare human beings who are able to express the inexpressible and transmit the intransmissible from many different
angles, so that it may penetrate on many levels of the reader's
awareness and make multiple living connections with his reader's
own insights. He never leads one astray into bogus mysticism or
esoteric symbolism; on the contrary, he cuts off all evasions, self-
indulgences, rationalizations, and conceptualizations, in order to
point directly at the self-nature, that Buddha Nature that we do
not 'have' but *are*, beyond the empirical ego. Suzuki attempts to
lead his reader to the great wisdom-compassion, to 'a realization

which is not self-realization, but realization pure and simple, beyond subject and object,' as Thomas Merton expressed it.

"To my mind Suzuki too was a Bodhisattiva, one who attained full enlightenment, then dwelt among those who search and suffer in order to offer them a glimpse of reality, of enlightenment. Neither he nor Pope John had a doctrine to teach, these men were the very doctrine they taught."

"Did you ever meet Suzuki?"

"In 1955 I visited him. I wondered if what I had gleaned from his books had any validity at all, or was it all nonsense? I had written down my thoughts to save him time, to impose as little as possible on him."

"What did he say?"

"He just gave me a radiant smile and said, 'It is not nonsense.'"

"I have noticed so often that if people dare to reveal their innermost concerns, their reality, if they speak from heart to heart, there is perfect understanding. All barriers fall away and communication is so easy."

"Your Holiness, I am amazed to feel at this moment not as if I were drinking coffee with . . . the Dalai Lama, but simply with a fellow human being. It makes me extremely happy and it gives me the courage to ask you, "Do you think it would be a useful experiment to X-ray, as it were, Christian concepts or rather insights, by means of Buddhist ones and vice versa? In this time of confusion and barbarism I can't think of anything that could be more important than the clarification of and reorientation towards the deepest existential insights the human spirit has achieved and which are hidden in the religions. I realize that it would be a huge task, a collective one. I have not the slightest illusion as to my personal adequacy or competence. But I am convinced in my very heart that such equivalents exist and that they are the key to a reorientation to what it means to be human."

The Dalai Lama said, "I believe not only that it is useful and think it is possible, but that in the present state of the world nothing indeed could be more important. A flawless understanding among the religions is not an impossible ideal. The followers of each religion should understand as much as possible of the religions of others precisely because in their deepest aspirations all religions, whatever their differences, point towards the same reality, the reality that lies at the root of every human being. You have my blessings!"

"I am very grateful," I said, "but excuse me if this sounds terribly rude, I always have difficulty with that word 'blessing'! It confuses me. Isn't it more or less your profession to bestow blessings? During the Vatican Council I drew all those bishops and cardinals and they were always blessing. I often asked myself, 'What on earth does it mean?' After all, it is even less expensive for popes and patriarchs to bless than for kings to give away titles and medals!"

He found this amusing and laughed aloud, "What is your own solution to the riddle?"

"Could a real blessing be that, knowing of one's own fullness of heart, one lets it overflow?"

"It might be giving, by knowing of the other's need. It is *upaya* (stratagem, skillful means). By the way, do you feel a little at home here, are you comfortable at the cottage?"

"Strange as it may seem, we feel completely at home. We come from the other side of the earth, don't speak a word of Tibetan, and after a week it feels as if we have lived here forever. We fell in love at first sight with your people."

"Maybe it is because you don't speak a word of Tibetan," he quipped.

Then he said gravely, "My people have lost everything, their country, their families, their homes, and they carry on. They are innocent people."

He spoke about the hardships of the refugees, their hardships in social and climatic readjustment, then he came back to the inner revolution among many of the young in the West.

"Is it really a revolution?" he wondered.

"I don't think revolution is really the right word. Maybe it is a mutation in awareness, which is something that takes place on a deeper level. It is the search of those who are no longer obsessed with technological utopias, but with the meaning of human life."

He said something in Tibetan to Tenzing Geiche, who disappeared and came back with the Dalai Lama's book *The Opening of the Wisdom Eye*. "This is quite elementary," he said, "but I also want to give you this."

It was a thin volume on Tantric meditation. Again he said something in Tibetan. Tenzing Geiche translated, "This book is given to very few people, whom his Holiness feels have a sincere and serious understanding of Buddhism."

The fourteenth Dalai Lama, Sakya Gejong Tenzin Gyatsho, then repeated it in English, took my hands and we both held the book. He also gave us a fine painted Tibetan *thanka* scroll.

As we left the modest palace and the dusk was blotting out the immense valley, a procession emerged from the Thekchen Choling, the Tibetan cathedral. Lamas in ox-blood red, pleated cloaks and cadmium yellow tricornered hats strode down the steps, preceded by an old abbot leaning on a staff, a yellow scarf over his deep red cloak. Young lamas blew silver shawms. Others carried sixteen-foot-long silver horns, the drums, cymbals, and bells and a large red stupa-shape, sculptured in butter. The procession moved solemnly down the narrow path to the entrance of the village where a tepee-shaped structure had been built of branches and leaves, then came to a halt. A young monk in a bright yellow and blue cloth apron and a white gauze scarf over his cloak brought offerings of water and apples. The chanting and the tellurian groans of the huge horns, accompanied by the shrill voices of the shawms, filled the thin mountain air. Old men and women prayed aloud, twirling cylindrical prayer wheels. It was nearly dark when the butter sculpture was placed inside the hut, which was then ignited. Flames shot up high into the deep-turquoise sky, consuming all the evil spirits and the worries of the past year. The New Year had started. In the blackness we stumbled down the steep path to the guesthouse.

On New Year's morning the valley was invisible from the terrace. A milk-white fog had settled over the world below. Through it we groped our way up the trail. Two young women in Sunday best, little flat velvet black hats on their tresses, climbed in front of us. One carried a baby in a red sling on her back. A grandfather in fur-lined top hat climbed with a four-year-old boy on his back. The old man was panting heavily. When his hat with the embroidered silk earflaps fell from his head, he put his load down and stood coughing for minutes. Then taking the boy on his back again he climbed on, praying aloud. Rain started to fall in hard straight drops. The wine red laurel blossoms glowed like jewel offerings of rubies. Drenched, we overtook four squat women with huge earrings. They wore poor Tibetan garb; at every fifth or sixth step they stopped, raised their arms wide, put their hands together, knelt and prostrated themselves completely in the mud, praying aloud. They shouted *"Tashi delé"* without interrupting their devout gymnastics.

The cathedral was overcrowded. The butter lamps before the feet of the seated Buddha were lit, lamas intoned sutras, accompanied by drums and horn blasts to announce and underline direct quotations of Buddha's holy words. On the right the image of Padma Sambhava (Tibetan: Guru Rimpoche) the Tantric Sage and founder of Tibetan Buddhism, on the left in a vast niche the image of Avalokitesvara, the Bodhisattva of Mercy, called Kwan Yin in China, Kwannon in Japan, and who as Chenresi is the patron saint of Tibet. His immense silver statue incorporates parts of the original sculpture from the Cathedral of Lhasa, sacked during the Chinese Cultural Revolution, when the sacred image was destroyed and thrown into the street. One peaceful and one wrathful face of Avalokitesvara were rescued and smuggled out of Tibet. The multi-armed statue is seated facing in the direction of Tibet, awaiting its return to Lhasa. On a table stood intricate butter sculptures as New Year offerings to the Buddha in scarlet, yellow, and blue. At the end of the service the Dalai Lama appeared on the terrace to greet the more than a thousand people waiting

Tibetan lamas with
the huge horns

in the rain in front of the cathedral. They lifted their children and waved the white gauze scarves that are signs of homage.

The Dalai Lama stood waving back at his faithful for a long time, the rain streaming down his shaven head, but his people had traveled from Ladakh, Sikkim, Nepal for this moment. Then he crossed the square among the waving scarves to his modest little palace.

On the verandah-like terrace of the temple, pilgrims continued to circumambulate. A blind Hindu beggar attempted pathetically to move the Tibetans to pity by melodramatic histrionics of misery, for which the stoic Tibetans have nothing but an instinctive revulsion. They turned away in embarrassment.

Our steep path had become a waterfall, the valley was still a solid mass of fog. We had slithered halfway down the slope when suddenly the immense opaque curtain started slowly to move from left to right. A second transparent veil behind it was drawn away and the sky appeared, a slate-blue slab with a magenta line running parallel to a world deep below that became gradually visible, valley after valley. The ochre rivers, the Tourist Hotel as a gleaming lump of sugar two thousand feet deep, a slow bus in a hairpin turn like an ant struggling uphill. . . The white mountains to the left were still hidden in a dark mist, but the valley lay in brilliant newborn sun. Two small grey birds with indigo wings skipped ahead from one rock to the next, we whistled softly, and they kept up the game, skipping, chirping, listening to our whistling, all the way to the sharp corner we already knew so well, the one where the high step comes and the unstable rock below.

The light that filters through the curtains this morning looks oddly pale. The terrace lies under two feet of snow. Beyond the snow, directly below, the valley stretches in dazzling green brocade with the pinks and whites of blooming trees. Behind the cottage the mountains rise as a wall of blinding white that disappears in swirling clouds. The evergreens are bent under heavy loads of snow. On leaking shoes I trudge up the trail, feeling for foothold on the rock-steps under the snow. The red laurel blooms are like carbuncles stitched on an ermine coat. I feel elated, yet slightly anxious, for I can't catch my breath. I am not that young! What if they should find me face down in the snow, carry me into the room where Claske is doing her hair. The climb takes twice as long as usual. I am close to the OM MANI PADME rock. Its red, yellow, white lettering stands above me against a tangle of white branches. Again I must stand still. I am thinking of nothing whatsoever, except how to catch my breath. I see the snow-laden branches and suddenly something utterly strange happens. As in a flash of lightning, I see. I just recall sitting down in the snow overwhelmed with some wild and quiet happiness until thoughts started to storm into a vacuum as air streams from a punctured can, in a feverish cascading commentary on what I had seen.

A century later, in front of the fire, I try to recall it for Claske. What I have seen or rather experienced in the "flash of lightning" seems now to be an enormous jump, a quantum leap across an abyss. I had seen a vision, had become that vision. This is all I can recall as an after-image of that vision. The commentary that rushed in like a storm or a waterfall I am perhaps better able to reconstruct, however inadequately.

I saw all living beings, and saw at work in each one of these beings some ruthless primeval narcissism, a pre-ego as it were, part of its biological equipment. I saw the pre-ego of the amoeba, which made it devour all that its pseudopodia could encompass, that of the plant, which let it push its branches towards the sun, unconcerned about its neighbors. In cockroaches and spiders I saw this pre-ego master complex stratagems like playing dead, in order to go on living. Pre-egos grazed in herds, hunted in packs, sought warmth in huddles. I saw myself as amoeba, as plant, as cockroach and spider, as innumerable forms of life that preceded me.

Then I saw myself: a human. I saw how my brain expanded, my intellect developed, manual dexterity was acquired and then, how something went awry. The pre-ego had become something else. No longer was it the animal pre-ego; it became perverted into something not yet human either. No longer satisfied with its role of maintaining the organism's integrity, it started to objectify itself, deluded itself as being independent, autonomous, even omnipotent. The primeval, purely biological animal narcissism had become fiercely psychological, the pre-ego became a protohuman ego, a not quite human Me. The intellect became parasitic, estranged me from my place in the cosmos, lost all connection with reality. In its delusions of grandeur it grew insanely competitive. It was an intellect, but pathetically incomplete and deficient, a defective computer.

A dog that steals a bone is happy with it. It does not consider itself a failure because another dog has stolen a steak. But my protohuman ego, in its defective self-awareness, compares compulsively. If, in its delusion of omnipotence, in its greed, the protohuman ego succeeded in conquering half the world, it would feel frustrated about the unconquered half. In its frustration the protohuman ego becomes aggressive, even murderous. Turned inward, this aggression leads to suicide or its substitutes, coronaries, ulcers, car collisions. Collectivized, our anger constantly snowballs into avalanches of cruelty, of terror, of mass psychosis, persecution, heresy hunt, total war, genocide. This protohuman ego, this atavistic embryonic protohumanity, is what we have mislabeled "human nature." As if it were anything but the hereditary defect of our self-destructive species.

The "leap" I saw, the "quantum jump," was that from a delusional protohuman nature to a mode of insight that is Specifically Human, that is, specific to the human species. At once it reintegrates Man into the cosmic reality. The protohuman ego, this empirical ego that in our delusion we take for "human nature"—a cultural hypothesis—suddenly stands naked as a malignant hypertrophy of what once was adequate as the animal's pre-ego. The intellectualized pretensions with which it defends and justifies its greed, its cruelty, stand revealed as the insane ignorance and delusion they are.

Jesus', Gautama's, every word and every act disclose that inside the human animal lives that which is Specifically Human. Ecce Homo! The quantum jump is not towards the outside, but towards the specifically human center of the heart. It is the jump from the first Adam of the Fall to the New Man who lies hidden in the center of the heart, as the oak lies hidden inside the acorn. It is the leap from *avidya* (cosmic ignorance) to the Original Face, to enlightenment, which is not some mystic's private delight but a radically realistic insight into our creaturely situation.

The empirical ego, the Me, when broken through and freed from its delusions, realizes its infinite interdependence and interrelatedness with all other selves in the cosmic fabric of the whole, above all realizes the transitoriness it shares with all other creatures and objects in the Structure of Reality, it becomes its self, the "I am before Abraham." This is Christ's *kenosis*, his self-emptying. Christ's crucifixion *is* his resurrection. Fall, kenosis, crucifixion, resurrection is the human Way, the Truth, and Life in Now/Here.

It is at a certain point in time that this quantum leap occurred in our species. Since that point our liberation from the protohuman has been demonstrated as being possible. Jesus does not claim extraordinary status in the cosmos, but he shows that the Kingdom is within Everyone. The Son of Man, points to the human kingdom within. The Buddha does not monopolize enlightenment; on the contrary, he points to the Liberator, the Saviour within and calls it "Bodhi," the Buddha-nature, which either is realized, Now/Here, or our human existence fails in achieving its ultimate human-divine meaning. "It is only the divine in man that justifies my belief in God," says Berdyaev.

From the moment of this mutation, this quantum jump from human delusion to human reality, our so-called "human-nature," that is still protohuman, has become atavistic. Insofar as I am still that protohuman ego, am still clinging to the Me, I am a throwback. For the true nature of man has been revealed, been made flesh.

This is the judgment that hangs over our species. Still we cling to our lives of spiritual dinosaurs. As such we are doomed.

This is what I could reconstruct in front of the fire.

What is this skidding of consciousness? When still a child I could coax something like it into happening by sitting quietly or walking slowly, focusing intensely on a tree, a cow, a cabbage, on falling snow, until something inside gave way and cabbage, snowfall, tree suddenly became three-dimensional or even multidimensional in a special way, as if seen through an ultrasharp lens or a stereopticon, each tree was seen growing from its own roots, becoming of infinite preciousness, pregnant with mystery and meaning.

Later, the experience became a passive one, no coaxing helped, one met oneself where least expected. Awareness skidded, as if from sleep to lucid waking, in momentary flashes, showing a reality that surpasses infinitely all sense data, not by denying but by intensifying them. When seen "multidimensionally," a human face is no longer either object or subject, or perhaps it is both object and subject. My eyes look through these eyes. The image on the retina needs no interpretation, is its own interpretation. The Me with all its criticisms, judgments, stereotypes, labels, has been suspended if only in a flash of grace; only joy—if that's the word—remains. Why call it anything? It happened, may happen again. Life is worth living.

Half a mile down the road to Dharamsala the grey mass of St. John's in the Wilderness with its blunt English Gothic tower stands surrounded by snow-laden trees and sagging tombstones—a Scottish Christmas card in the Himalayas. Here lie the soldiers killed by the earthquake of 1905, which destroyed the entire Scottish garrison of McLeod Ganj. Suddenly, noiselessly, a tribe of huge grey monkeys with white starched collars under black faces invades the cemetery, leaps from tombstone to tombstone. I count thirty, forty; the leader takes a menacing jump in my direction, then crouches. For an instant we probe each other's faces. Then he turns around contemptuously, leaps back over the tombstones followed by his underlings. The graveyard is empty, again a sentimental calendar picture of Auld Lang Syne.

It is almost dark as I reach our cottage, but we still go for a walk along the narrow path that runs from the guesthouse parallel to the abyss, across neolithic-looking stone bridges built from boulders, that span crystal rivulets. We call it "the French path" after a beloved path near Magagnosc in Provence.

Deep below in the valley, lights are twinkling. Claske picks up a dead bird among the leaves. The Buddha married too young. He left his wife when he was twenty-eight. He missed knowing the married path, where not only bodies and minds, but even the eyes can become one.

We arrived here eons ago, lived for generations in the cottage above the valley. Chodon cooked thick soups, little Tenshe played timelessly on the terrace. New York, Holland became vague dreams. Here we would live and die and live again till the great conflagration at the end of the world.

But already we carry our luggage down the path to the bus stop near the Tourist Hotel in Dharamsala.

Hong Kong Harbor

﹡ *Hong Kong—Tokyo* ﹡

The roar of the Boeing rising over Delhi into the stratosphere decodes the origin of Indian spirituality, of Vedanta and the Upanishads. Either perish in this cauldron of suffering, this flaming world of birth, growing pains, business, dissolution, death, or rise above it! A few men, desperate but lucid, endowed with high intelligence, saw this only escape, constructed themselves spiritual Boeings, turned the switch, and contemptuous of all lethal dangers, disregarding the laws of gravity, lifted themselves through layers of pollution, through blankets of foul cloud, into the limpid transparency of silence, into Wisdom and Compassion.

"On your left," drawls the Texan pilot through the intercom, "on your left, ladies and gentlemen, you see Mount Everest."

In an infinity of pale swallow-egg blue, as if drawn in liquid pink-gold, the mythic mountain of mountains stands, on a lacquered tray of dove-grey clouds. A perfect piece of precious kitsch? A mother-of-pearl Eiffel Tower? Iceberg of Emptiness in the ocean of Emptiness?

Now/Here. Orange juice, babies crying, sucking. A man in a loud tartan sports jacket puts his arm around a compliant stewardess. They grin like sheep. The jet whisper-roars at 37,000 feet. Below, a mud-colored estuary, a strip of beach and sea. Laconically the loudspeaker drawls again, "Ladies and gentlemen, we are now over Vietnam. This is the Mekong Delta."

The stewardess puts my lunch tray in front of me. Bon appetit. "White wine or red?"

Time stands still until the sky has lost all brilliance. We are floating in limpid lustreless powder-blue emptiness.

We lose altitude, dive sharply between wisps, then tatters, of steel-grey, into a cloud-sea that changes from lead-grey to

charcoal, fall deeper and deeper into a bottomless well of
blackness. Dead stillness roars through the fuselage. Are we
dropping endlessly into nothingness? Suddenly lights, a million lights. We have fallen out of daylight into depth of night.
From night into light. The light is Hong Kong.

An after-image of Hong Kong: a neo-Oriental San Francisco;
Kowloon: an Asian Bronx. Yet in the fishing suburb of Aberdeen
the Hong Kong of the late, late movie still exists, the Hong Kong
of sinister alleys, huts, dingy hotels, markets, narrow dirty
streets hung with laundry drying on bamboo poles around a
dirty bay choked with dilapidated houseboats, clusters of brown
tarred junks with Chinese doll-children playing on the high
square poops. Tiny covered ferries are sculled by women standing on the stern, rotating long bamboo poles. On decayed
wooden jetties old crones with impassive parchment faces,
dressed in black padded jackets, sit behind baskets of tiny sil-
very fish, shrimp, and conches, waiting for Humphrey Bogart to
pick up the opium.

*The hydrofoil bumps across the mouth of the Pearl River to Macao,
that cynical joke of the nightmare called history, that puny six square
miles of Portuguese scab on the nose of the People's Republic of China,
unscratched as long as it is useful. A Portuguese provincial town of
decaying, shuttered houses, crumbling archways and buttresses in all
varieties of bastardized baroque and rococo, decaying facades orna-
mented with garlands of fruit, lion's claws, arabesques, crucifixes,
cherubs and madonnas in peeling lavender, paled cobalt blues, and
weathered copper greens, faded pinks and purples. A labyrinth of cobblestoned alleys, drooping wharves, tottering godowns, corroded rail-
ings, disintegrated staircases.*

Behind the altar of San Agostinho stands a life-size wax figure of
Christ dressed in a brand new wine-red velvet cloak.
Sadomasochistic wax tears and blood trickle from below the
crown of thorns, the glass eyes are all soul. An old Chinese

woman, bent double with arthritis, reverently paws the cloak
three times with clawed fingertips.

The Makok Miu, a fisherman's shrine on the water's edge, is old
China. Here the devotees, businesslike, place burning incense
sticks in braziers filled with sand, in the gaping maws of dragons and of stone temple dogs. In the main temple business is
brisk. A kiosk sells paper offerings to old women who burn
these tentlike paper contraptions wholesale on the central altar,
sprinkle purifying water. A crone in worn black trousers shakes
a box of sticks for her farmer-type client, tells him the result and
starts haggling over her payment.

A dozen blind beggars stand close together, chattering and
laughing. An old woman of classical dignity pays obeisance at
every one of the shrines, enters the main temple, and gets busy
gathering paper offerings for the altar. Her white hair is severely
pulled back, the citron yellow skin is taut over the sharp cheek-
bones, her eyes are turned inward. She lights her offerings with
gravity, then gropes in her handbag for a cigarette and lights it
at the holy flame, sucking in her cheeks.

The gods don't mind. It is not part of the deal.

*Across the harbor, on the marshes in front of the grey ochre hills, Red
Chinese soldiers stand under iron umbrellas in front of concrete sentry
boxes in the drizzle. Fast Chinese gunboats plow through the murky
water.*

*On a hilltop, high above the city, stands the seventeenth-century empty
facade of the Cathedral of São Pãolo, built on rock. The church burned
a hundred years ago. Behind, below, beyond the empty window holes
spreads the endless void of sky above hills, roof tiles, rococo ornaments,
and the masts of junks.*

*The facade in flamboyant Jesuit baroque is a surfeit of gargoyles and
pilasters, friezes, and capitals, but its heart is formed by a glorious bas-
relief of the Dove of the Holy Spirit. Its church long gone, unmissed,
the haughty empty facade has weathered all wars, uprisings, and*

typhoons; it will endure for centuries, a majestic front for emptiness, an indestructible icon of transiency, imprinted with the Dove. I must send a picture postcard to Rome.

Above Japan the sun is setting appropriately, a blood-red disk in a white sky. The Dai-Ichi Hotel in Tokyo ("Wide-up Dai-Ichi" it says on the matchbook in matchless Japanese English) is a super-Sheraton, more station than hostelry. The vast lobby is crowded with men in navy blue suits and white shirts, women in either miniskirts or kimonos. Whatever the uniform, all bow to one another, legs together, hands on knees, broken at the waist in 90-degree angles, bow again, again, again. The reception desk processes guests in record time. The smiling bellhops have already grabbed one's luggage, don't expect tips. The room is like a tourist-class ship's stateroom, eight by eight and spotless: slippers stand ready, fresh *yukatas,* light cotton kimonos, lie on the beds, in the thermos waits hot green tea. Between the beds a panel controls the six lights, the radio, the television. Double windows insulate one from the din outside in dulled stillness. The mini-bathroom has a mini-bathtub of immaculate plastic, a mini-refrigerator for mini-icecubes. Plastic signs, with cartoons, explain the use of shower and basin. Above the toilet bowl are pictorial directions for use. Japanese unfamiliar with Western toilet bowls have been known to clamber on seats, squat, slide off slippery plastic, break skulls against towel hooks.

Outside the double window lies the metropolitan landscape of agony. Fourteen floors below, trains rush noiselessly over viaducts. A building is going up in the middle distance. Radio towers, superimposed on girder skeletons, make op-art patterns of steel. At 8:30 A.M. a blanket of polluted wetness lies over the crowd that emerges from the earth at Shimbashi subway station, legions of punch-card men in the identical navy blue with white shirts, neat black hair, and briefcases. Bandy-legged girls in short skirts, flat heels come in three standardized faces: round, medium, concave. Innumerable pairs of identical black narrow eyes stare, unseeing, into their line of motion. Every tenth face wears a surgical mask.

At the station, the crowds are denser than at the Times Square subway station during rush hour. Tickets are pulled from banks of automatic machines; destinations, fares are indicated above the automats. At the gates, men in peaked caps punch tickets, twirl their pincers between punches with high virtuosity. No one pushes, struggles, shouts, talks. All submit to being carried along, passively, unaggressively, resigned to the fate of human molecules, perfected in adaptability.

Between the skyscrapers, their entire facades covered with garish advertising signs, a triangular little square has been left as by oversight. Seven real trees grow out of the concrete around an atrocious abstract sculpture that advertises Seiko ("Success") watches. Dense traffic rushes around this pseudo-oasis in the clanging, crashing, roaring audiovisual hell of the metropolis.

In a concrete miniature pond behind the monstrous sculpture two white ducks are swimming rapidly, frenziedly. A thin woman in black kimono throws food that they gobble swiftly, unable to stop in their overstimulated agitation. Two little boys discover the ducks, watch them in exultation with yells of high excitement. A derelict in tatters stares transfixed, kneels at the low parapet, talks to the ducks in a shrill throaty whisper. Kyrie Eleison.

The taxi is brand new and gleaming as are all Tokyo taxis. The driver in navy blue wears one white glove, opens the automatic door by a lever under the dashboard, closes it behind me. Silent, ramrod-stiff, he maneuvers his taxi with virtuosity, dodges buses, Datsuns, Mazdas, Toyotas, bicycles. The radio, full blast, vomits commercials I cannot understand for the full twenty minutes of the ride. The bought voices rattle in the same spurious intimacy, contemptible joviality, counterfeit heartiness, as they do in English, French, Hindi, Italian, Dutch. A million advertising signs fly past in black, red, royal blue. I have no inkling what they advertise, what they want me to desire with all my heart, what they want me to buy, to fear. Loudspeakers mounted on trucks carrying large photographs of politicians, mix with the car-radio's din. How mercifully deaf, blind, mute, illiterate I am! The entire apparatus designed to warn me of imaginary risks to my health, to create my cravings, to determine choices between brands of soap-powder, cigarettes, and cars dashes to pieces against this blessed deaf and blind illiteracy. The coaxing voices, the glad tidings of the lettered signs are all in vain, empty, powerless stimuli. Inside all remains tranquil, unalienated.

The taxi stops. The driver grins "Bye! Bye!"

At the suburban station a silent, solid torrent of human flesh sucks one along to the platform. The crowd moves mutely. Loudspeakers have the floor and blare constant streams of information and instruction. The line of would-be taxi riders outside the station is two blocks long, the traffic-rush around the station unbroken. Two clanging iron footbridges cross the street, separated from the sidewalk by guard rails. In a flash of interruption in the traffic stream I see five large rats flattened on the pavement, blood still gleaming.

Stephen Lynch, O.F.M., at the new, aseptic Franciscan Chapel Center, says, "If you can show equivalents in the Eastern and Western spiritual traditions, more power to you! People are hungry for meaning and if meaning has evaporated in one place, then for God's sake let's look for it where it still exists, wherever we find it. Let the theologians fight about the fine distinctions, after all that's their living!"

I quote a friend, a campus chaplain in New Jersey:

"These kids are desperate for meaning, they gobble up anything that promises it: psychological literature, Fromm, Laing, Perls, all the Swamis, Maharishis, Yogis, Zen Masters, astrologers, shamans, and Kahlil Gibran! As long as you don't sound institutionally Christian, as long as you don't quote Scripture, as long as what you have to say is based on personal experience, you'll be all right, they'll read it."

Lynch continues, "Only basics matter now. Just listen to the texts of the rock songs, where a whole generation sings its heart out. Blessed are the parents who listen to the music of their teen-

agers, for they shall gain some understanding of the fearful
world in which their children live and move. One song goes,
'No one would care, no one would cry, if I should live or die.' If
that isn't the song of alienation, rejection, depersonalization,
dehumanization! But perhaps this is the precondition for understanding once more the command to love one another, to look
into one's neighbors' eyes and behold the face of Christ."

He quotes from J. D. Salinger's *Franny and Zooey*, "The Jesus
prayer has one aim only, to endow the person who says it with
Christ consciousness."

"I would say 'make aware of' instead of 'endow,' Father, for
this Christ Consciousness has been there all the time; it doesn't
fall from the sky. I see it as the equivalent to what the Mahayana
Buddhists call Buddha Nature. Essential Christianity and essential Buddhism seem to meet somewhere here. Both point at a
hidden, yet univocally present, specifically human mode of
awareness."

"Salinger," says Fr. Lynch, "lets Zooey say, 'Who in the whole
Bible besides Jesus knew—actually *knew*—that we're carrying
the kingdom around with us, inside, where we're really too stupid and sentimental and unimaginative to look?'"

"A Mahayana Christianity, Father, might be our only alterna-
tive to total barbarism!"

Do I happen to meet whom I *have to* meet, steered by mysterious affinities? By chance introductions?

Dr. Kondo Akihisa is about sixty. Before the War he had been a
businessman. Drafted into the army, he broke a leg during basic
training. His contingent was shipped overseas while he was con-
valescing. The troop ship went down near Formosa and all his
buddies were drowned. For Kondo Akihisa this was the turning
point. He would not go back to business, vowed to devote his life
to something more useful. He studied medicine, then took
courses at Columbia in the early fifties and became a psychiatrist.

"One can only liberate patients from their hangups to the
degree one is oneself liberated. I have treated many priests and

missionaries with nervous breakdowns, often in conflict with their superiors, who feared I would kill their faith, convert them to Buddhism. All I did was to open up their own vacuum-sealed Christian symbolism to them! They had often no idea at all, had hardly thought of the deeper meaning of their Christian symbolism, of the rites they perform every day. When I explained the meaning of 'original sin' as primal ignorance, delusion, the split between subject and object, they were astonished, fascinated. They had usually thought of it in terms of some historical curse they inherited, something vaguely connected with nudity, masturbation, sex. I didn't have the slightest desire to convert these men, but religion is either a terrible poison, or that which helps to keep us sane!

"According to Buddhist understanding, our existential state of suffering comes out of two kinds of ignorance inseparably related. First is our ignorance of the fact that we are alienated from our deepest ground, our Buddha Nature, which is the True Self. Secondly our ignorance of the presence of this Bodhi, the Buddha Nature, in ourselves, in every human being. We are simply ignorant of our ignorance of the Buddha Nature we are born with. So we surrender blindly without any point of orientation to instinctual impulses governed roughly, in Freud's terms, by the principles of pleasure and death. The more we are driven by these impulses, the more we pursue their fulfillment, even with our reason resisting by means of repression, the more alienated we become from the real self. Do you follow me?"

"Isn't it remarkable," I said, "that this is the second time today that someone, the first one was an American Catholic priest, states my own central conviction. Father Lynch called what you call Buddha Nature, Christ Consciousness. To me Christ Nature and Buddha Nature, if not synonymous, are at any rate highly analogous. When I talk to young people I feel that there is something like a meta-Christianity in the air; the post-Christian era might still become meta-Christian or call it Mahayana Christian with the Christ Consciousness as our central point of faith, perhaps the only one! It would in no way be a substitute religion!"

Dr. Kondo said, "I see that you understand what my psychotherapy is based on. I attach little value to psychiatric or, for that matter, national or religious labels. Human beings have to realize their reservoir of sanity and health, call it their Buddha Nature, call it Christ Consciousness, by awakening to what is nothing but a perception of reality, of things as-they-are, by transcending the dichotomy between ego and true self, in other words, by awakening as a whole human being. One could also say, by discovering the 'reality principle' within, beyond the pleasure and death principles. To experience this is to help others towards experiencing it. This is the spiritual life Zen points at. Only by reaching this reality principle, the wholeness and integration within oneself, can one help others. At the very point where Freud's diagnosis of the existential state of mankind ends in pessimism, Zen finds its positive doctrine of liberation. In my work with the priests it is the opening-up of their own Christian myths and symbols which helps them to liberate themselves from their hang-ups."

Suddenly he asked, "What do you make of the Genesis myth? Why does God throw Adam and Eve out of Eden? It always puzzles me."

I had the impression the question was a test.

"He didn't even have to," I said. "Once you have eaten from the Tree of Knowledge, have acquired the know-how, the pseudoknowledge which makes you see your 'Me' as absolute, makes you 'hide your nakedness,' you are estranged from reality, from the Bodhi-ground, the Christ Consciousness, the Specifically Human self-awareness, the True Self. At that very moment you are, without any special divine intervention, dispossessed of Eden, and fall into the grip of karma. The Me cannot eat from the Tree of Life which feeds the True Self."

Kondo said, "Even enlightenment does not nullify karma. In the words of the ancient story of the man who was changed into a fox, when he asserted that the enlightened man is not subject to karma, 'The enlightened man does not stand in the way of his karma.'

"Jesus is such a man," he added. "Jesus accepts his karma, inclusive of his death on the cross, that, according to legend, was made out of the wood of the 'Tree of Life.' Hence he is transfigured, is the Liberator."

It was as if we had known one another from childhood as neighbors. We spoke the same language, no "cultural barriers" were left.

The tickets come out of a computerized machine, complete with the imprint: car 11, seats E and F. On the platform where an 11 is painted on the pavement, we join a line. At 11:54 the train arrives. The doors open. At 11:55 it is empty. A swarm of charwomen and cleaners stands ready to attack the train with brooms, cloths, vacuum cleaners. The doors close behind them. At 11:58 the doors open once more. At 11:59 we are all seated in spotless aluminum and royal blue velvet. Not a wrapper on the floor, not a match in the ashtrays. At 12 sharp the train moves. Men in dark blue with white shirts, women mostly in suits, a few in kimonos, sit in silence. Without a trace of vibration the train glides over high viaducts between immense neon signs. We slither through endless suburbs, through a disconsolate landscape of cranes, smokestacks, trash heaps, high-tension wires, complex bridges, elevated highways, stop for one minute at Yokohama, flow further for one hour and a half to Nagoya. The landscape remains that of the no-man's land between the Holland Tunnel and Newark. Between industrial plants, clusters of brown-grey houses huddle along narrow alleys without any attempt at planning. Levittowns are luxury estates by comparison.

At last the train glides through wild mountain country, through long tunnels, between high embankments, here and there broken by valleys planted with tea, then again through endless complexes of factories and giant neon signs with hardly a hint of vegetation. Between the haphazardly strewn factories children play on forgotten triangles of land, pockmarked ochre clay with persistent tufts of tough grass. Canals run in concrete conduits, poison-green with pollution. At Nagoya the train stops for two minutes. A temple compound stands dwarfed by huge electrical installations. Mount Fuji is visible today, through translucent smog. The gigantic cone of the sacred mountain, covered with snow, rises out of a tangle of bridges, smokestacks, cranes, apartment houses. Bandy-legged girls in smart uniforms come around with coffee, ice cream, lunchboxes of sushi. All chew and drink with trained dignity, then carry their empty boxes, paper cups, wrappers, and paper napkins silently to a flap for trash disposal.

The train crosses a hilly landscape, slopes covered with snowy pines. In fields and frozen rice paddies the commonplace matchbox houses stand in their haphazard bunches. Here and there in a flash, an old Japanese style house is visible until obscured by enormous advertising signs along the tracks. After three hours the train stops at Kyoto.

Island shrine Izumo, Japan

⚘ *Kyoto* ⚘

The new cities, the suburbs of America, England, France, Italy, Holland, India, Japan, Hong Kong are unrelated to human need, human reality, spirit, life. Totally deficient in what the old cities have in abundance, they lack architectural and human differentiation, atmosphere, fail to stimulate and nourish the imagination. They are the perfect expression of a totalitarian perversion that provides cages for dehumanized cattle, overpopulated, uninhabitable places of exile, joyless deserts in which there is nothing to be experienced and where television and mechanical noise and violence offer the substitute for a life not lived, a death not died. There is no force strong enough to defeat the institutionalized egoism, barbarism, cynicism, and contempt that impose this environment on humans who lost—exploiters and exploited alike—all criteria of what it means to be human. Only a turning around at the base could break this tyranny of heartlessness, where people are tolerated only as auxiliaries to industrial enterprise.

Two chance meetings brought me to Kyoto. In the jet from New York to Vienna a few years ago, I sat next to a round-faced middle-aged Japanese gentleman whom I took to be a businessman. I was reading the sutra of Hui-Neng. After some hours my neighbor could not contain himself and expressed amazement at my reading material. For the remaining six hours we talked Buddhism. Yoshinori Takeuchi, professor of Buddhist Philosophy at the University of Kyoto, was on his way to the World Philosophical Congress in Vienna.

A bit later, during the Tillich lectures at New Harmony, Indiana, as a guest of Ms Jane Blaffer Owen, I shared a cottage with Professor Masatoshi Doi. Professor Doi, born a Buddhist, was baptized at nineteen, studied theology at Kyoto's Doshisha University and the Chicago Theological and Hartford seminaries. In Kyoto he combines the directorship of the Center for the Study of Japanese Religions of the National Council of Churches with a professorship at Doshisha, and has translated Paul Tillich into Japanese. During the daily debates at New Harmony he seemed a meditative island of silence, but during the nights we had long, delightful talks in our cozy cottage. And now I am in Kyoto, with the NCC Center for the Study of Japanese Religions as headquarters.

Presiding over a meeting of the cream of Japanese philosophers, Doi is the erudite discussion leader; behind his desk at the Center one might take him for a bureaucrat. In his rustic bungalow, dressed in kimono, he cooks a superb sukiyaki, becomes charming host, humorous sage. Buddhist and Christian values have conducted a lifelong debate within him. Interfaith dialogue is his natural vocation.

On a wintry Sunday morning, I had promised to join some new friends at a Protestant Church, 1905 neo-Gothic, a mile north of the Palace. An interior with whitewashed walls. The congregation, middle-aged and upper-middle-class Japanese, sings its hymns dutifully, bows its heads when expected. The youngish minister delivers an interminable sermon in grave monotone, standing stiffly behind his lectern, his face an unchanging frown. His right fist rests on the bible in front of him. At regular intervals he hits the holy book with a sharp karate chop.

My friend translates: "God calls upon us through the Cross of Christ . . . died for us, sinners. . . . Saint Paul . . . road to Damascus. . . . Foundation for hope . . . stumbling block to human reason . . ."

Final karate chop.

A Japanese behavioral pastiche of a Midwestern Sunday morning, unbroken continuum of voice-noise, of word chains, of collective bellowing linked by organ tinkling. Are there any foreign markets left for this ready-made called "worship"?

Nehan-Eh, March 15, is the anniversary ceremony of the Buddha's death in 485 B.C. In Tofokuji, the oldest temple of the Zen sect in Kyoto, a few miles southeast of Kyoto Station, the famous sixteenth-century scroll depicting the passing of Siddhartha Gautama Sakyamuni into *nehan* or nirvana, into liberation, is shown during the Nehan-Eh. It was painted by Mincho, a famous painter-priest of the Muromachi period.

Tofokuji, a large temple complex, stands forlorn in the snow. The Daibutsu-Den Hall, open on all sides, is nearly deserted. On stocking feet a few shivering figures shuffle over the tatami-covered floor. On a raised platform seven elderly nuns in black kimonos with purple and white piping are kneeling *suwari*-style on cushions, holding the ceremonial bell with the *vajra* handle in the right hand, striking it rhythmically while reciting an endless sutra. A very ancient, wizened nun fingers a large brown wooden rosary. The hall looks festive. Purple and white banners are swaying from the high, coffered ceiling. Mincho's painting covers a whole wall. It is a bright scroll, some fifty feet high. In a moonlit landscape among eight tall trees Gautama lies on his side, surrounded by fifty or sixty human figures in attitudes of mourning, joined by all the animals of the forest. Elephant, bull, tiger, and leopard are weeping, their heads thrown back, a lion near the center sobs pitifully. Mincho even included the cat, usually excluded from the iconography because of its reputation of unfaithfulness.

Six men enter in stocking feet, kneel down on the tatamis in front of the scroll, unwrap wide bamboo flutes and blow a shrill, melancholy dirge as a musical offering to the Buddha. Then they get up and leave as silently as they have come.

In the yellow light of the bumping old bus to Arashiyama, full of working people, schoolgirls in sailor suits, high-school boys in flat peaked caps and dark grey uniforms with brass buttons, I forget I look foreign. Why was I not born here? Two stout women across the aisle are gossiping with international female gestures about some exasperating absentee. At Arashiyama a sign points to Seirijoji Temple. A balloon vendor hurries ahead, streetlights suffuse his scarlet, mauve, lemon-yellow jewels. Gradually the road becomes crowded between stalls selling ricecakes, sushi, pickled vegetables, fruit, spun sugar, candied apples, tempura. At the massive temple gate there is a crush.

Kwannon, Bodhisattva of Mercy, Sanjusangendo.

Three enormous torches, built of tree trunks and pinebranches, stand waiting in the muddy temple grounds where goldfish-fishing contests are in progress, and batteries of slot machines are overworked. Hawkers sell fans, paper snakes, firecrackers, salty seaweed cookies. Groups of boys pursue covens of giggling girls; the ubiquitous grandfathers on wooden clogs drag their inevitable grandchildren. Nowhere a hint of boisterousness, of vandalism. The moment is sweet; let's not spoil it!

In the center of the hall, where Seirijoji's Buddha is on view this one day of the year, the bearded abbot in splendid gold miter and purple and gold robe nears the end of his sermon. He blinks through round owl glasses, makes ample stylized gestures, then with drums and gongs pounding, solemnly, and surrounded by priests in stiff gold and black robes, he strides to the Nehan-zu, the painting of Sakyamuni's passing, contemplates it, and makes gestures of blessing.

Around the braziers little boys, cold from their goldfishing contests, stand warming themselves. The huge temple bell booms constantly. Young men swing the wooden clapper that hangs in the low belfry with all their might, proving their strength. The crowd is waiting tensely.

The priests, flanked by men carrying huge paper lanterns on long poles, start to march around the twenty-foot-high torches. Simultaneously three huge sheets of flame leap into the night sky, throw showers of sparks. The crowd roars in delight. Firemen and police watch both conflagration and crowd, take no chances.

In this Otaimatsu-Shiki, one of the oldest surviving rituals, the torches represent three different kinds of rice. The promise of the harvest for each type in the current year is divined by the force of the fire symbolizing it.

In the temple the red paper lanterns are still burning, but the hall is empty. The golden Buddha, brought here centuries ago from India via China, sits all alone, smiling at the apples, the water, the rice brought to him as offerings.

Dragon, Kyomizodera, Kyoto

Buddhist pilgrims, Rokokudo

In the park of the Kyoto National Museum, Rodin's The Thinker, *head in hand, sits frowning, as he does internationally, at the Musee Rodin, at the Amsterdam and the Philadelphia museums.*

But in the Reihokan, the treasure house of Koryuji Temple, smiles the Miroku Bosatsu, exquisitely slender seventh-century wood sculpture of the Buddha Maitreya, the Buddha yet to come. The torso is inclined forward, much like that of Rodin's Thinker, but how different they are! The Thinker is wracking his brain, Miroku thinks with his entire body. The Thinker frowns, Miroku smiles his beatific smile; his head needs no support, the right hand is gracefully curved below the chin, middle finger and thumb barely touching.

Is this the difference between reductive thinking and transcendental insight, between intellection and intuition? Or between knowledge and wisdom, between worrisome preoccupation and enlightened bliss? It would be too simplistic to see it as the contrast between East and West, for at last these have met. All too thoroughly. Professor Takeuchi, who has taken me to see the Miroku-Bosatsu, contemplates the sculpture for a long time. Then he says, "Seeing him, you see!"

This Miroku-Bosatsu, as do all the great authentic works of art, speaks from the self to the self, speaks about and to the center of the heart more directly than the Scriptures. A Rembrandt drawing of a face does not move me because it is the likeness of a face that died three hundred years ago, but because beyond that likeness Rembrandt has seen what is centrally human, the Original Face of a man who never dies. His nudes do not portray some particular naked woman, but witness the centrally human in its female manifestation, in ineffable compassion. In the Art of the Fugue, in the Misericordia of the "Magnificat," in a hundred other works, an avatar, a Christophany called Bach spells out limpidly, clearly what the Scriptures confound in words. Many people who cringe at the mere thought of a church service are profoundly, "religiously," stirred by the

Great Buddha of Nagoya

Goldberg Variations and Mozart Masses, experience the centrally human, the cosmic, the divine.

A haze of green covers the trees on the mountain across the cascading Hozu River, at Arashiyama. Pointed wooden pleasure boats are sculled upstream by strong boatmen, their passengers sit under the flat roofs eating bowls of noodles. Tortuous pinetrees overhang the banks. From an open-air restaurant comes flute music. Think away the cars and here is the Japan of Hiroshige.

Still, the famous temple garden of Tenryuji, with its vast pond in the shape of the Chinese character for heart, *kokoro*, looks self-satisfied and dead. It has been here since the fourteenth century. Has it been adored too long? Not a bird, not an insect stirs, the garden is congealed. Then, walking back to the gate, through an open door I see on a white wall a particularly fine scroll painting of Bodhidarma, the first prophet-patriarch who imported Zen from India to China.

Below the scroll in a vase stands a blossoming branch. A tiny first leaf of tenderest green peers out of a gleaming hairy bud on this amputated branch.

Michiko Kimura, the assistant librarian, who makes me feel like a giant, has a degree in English literature. When I am working at the university library, she noiselessly puts green tea at my elbow, and talks. She has a finely organized mind, complex and profound thought processes. Every day she travels from Osaka, which she despises, to Kyoto, practices Zen meditation at Daitokuji Temple every week and takes *cha-no-yu*, tea ceremony lessons in a Buddhist nunnery on Wednesday evenings. I am invited to join her for one of her lessons. On entering the nunnery, Michiko—she is tiny, twenty-five—puts on clean white knee socks. A beautifully becalmed old nun is the tea-mistress. Her skull is clean-shaven. In her charcoal-grey kimono she carefully follows every movement of her pupils in the tiny tea room, pervaded by a faint fragrance of incense. Besides Michiko-san there

The Teamistress, Buddhist Nun.

are two girls in miniskirts and the serious young man who
screeched to a stop in his red sports Mazda when we arrived. He
and Michiko-san are advanced students. The tea-mistress is all
attention, criticizes the amplitude of an arm movement as the
young man wipes the teabowl before replacing it in its preor-
dained position, gestures to correct the turning of the black Raku
ceramic teabowl while he presents it to the guest. As Michiko-
san, who is in her third year of study, prepares for her turn, a
shadow moves on the paper screen of the sliding door. A third
girl kneels in the door opening, bows from her kneeling position
until her head touches the floor, silently slides to an empty cushion. Michiko's face is closed in inwardness. Her every movement
has become of infinitely tender precision. The placing of the siz-
zling kettle back on the brazier, the contemplation of the wooden
ladle that will scoop the boiling water into the bowl, have
become acts of tender devotion, absolute precision. She had
brought her own tea caddy, a red and gold lacquered heirloom,
protected by an embroidered glove. Michiko-san is no longer a
librarian. She is no longer Michiko-san, she is the priestess
clothed in *wabi*, in solitariness, in tranquillity, poverty, and gentleness of spirit.

She has become who she is. The deep obeisance, the reverence
with which she offers me the teabowl is no longer either a personal nor an impersonal, but a transpersonal homage. Michiko's
ego-mask has evaporated, she has become intensified, mysteriously centered; she has become her Self. Hence she is now Joshu,
a Master who lived during the Tang dynasty.

A monk came to Joshu, who asked:

"Have you been here before?"

"No, Master," answered the monk.

Joshu said: "Have a cup of tea."

Another monk came in. Again Joshu asked:

"Have you been here before?"

"Yes, Master," he replied.

"Have a cup of tea," said Joshu.

This is *cha-no-yu*, the eucharist of Zen.

Arashiyama

Joshu has become Michiko again as we walk through the drizzle that creates a nimbus around each street lamp and makes Kyoto as familiar as New York or Utrecht.

A week ago along the Kamo River the trees were still bare, today under sweeps of newborn willow green and cherry blossoms, the lovers sit on the rocks at the water's edge. In the narrow streets between the river and Higashijo Avenue there must be fifty temples, but I search in vain for the particular one where I have seen a courtyard, covered entirely by the branches of a marvelously trained ancient pine tree. I can't find it. Every temple compound I walk into today seems behexed, a congested parking lot. A loudspeaker truck crawls behind me, yelling the same shrill slogan over and over again. I wander through a derelict cemetery where tall wooden memorial tablets clatter in the tepid wind, into a lovely, neatly kept temple garden. A wizened monk in dirty kimono is raking the gravel into wavy patterns around two yard-high rocks.

"The money that used to go into temples now goes into cars, radios, vacuum cleaners, office buildings," he complains.

A little boy in neon-red baseball cap bursts into the garden with his machine gun. "Ratatatatat!" he goes, "ratatatat!"

In the Japan of my experience there seems hardly an oasis left. Even the shrines and temples are choked by exploding crowds with radios and cameras. Yet within these reservations there remain inner sanctuaries, islands of silence, carefully walled-in and bolted, where Japan keeps its fine-grained spirit intact.

Daitokuji Temple, one of the important temples of Rinzai Zen, is a huge compound at Murasakino in northern Kyoto. In streaming rain I search desperately for one of the many auxiliary temples, Ryuko-in, am late for my appointment with Nanrei Kobori, the Zen Master. At last a young monk shows me the way. Across courtyards and long cobblestoned walks, behind a hidden gate, lies the short path to the entrance. The translucent white paper

screen almost instantly splits open. A young monk who sits in
suwari in the door opening, bows to the ground. Kicking off my
shoes, I follow him over highly polished planks, past a superb
ink painting of partridges, to a small, almost empty room.
Nanrei Kobori must be about forty-five. His face, very much
alive, is sparingly modeled in flesh stretched nearly translu-
cently over the structure of the skull. His eyes are large, his
movements precise, deliberate, aristocratically courteous. His
English is fluent but carefully wrought, so that the sentences
seem to mold themselves in a poetic medium. Kobori was a student of Daisetz Suzuki.

"As an apostle of Buddhism," I say, "he was a Saint Paul to
the gentiles."

"Suzuki," says Kobori, whisking green tea in a heavy, ancient
black teabowl of Miro-like design, "was the woodcutter in a virgin forest. Don't forget, he was not an academic philosopher but
studied literature and taught English, not philosophy. As a
young man he was not an enthusiastic student at all, but he
always was the meditator. He practiced Zazen intensively, nearly
desperately. When he was a student at Waseda University in
Tokyo, he walked thirty miles to Kamakura to practice Zen
under Abbot Kosen Roshi, who died in his presence in 1892.
Then he continued under his successor Shaku Soen. He reached
kensho, the first glimpse into self-nature, in 1896.

"Then he went to America where the process continued. As he
said himself, 'I became conscious of what it was I had experienced.' He succeeded in his great ambition, namely to make the
reality of Zen accessible to the Western way of thinking without
perverting it, without killing it. His thought never hardened into
an ideology, never became the logical outcome of a certain way
of scientific or metaphysical thinking, it always came directly
out of his own spiritual experience. He did not approach reality
from the outside, he truly became one with the reality of what
he called the 'cosmic unconscious' which lies at the root of all
existences and unites all in the oneness of Being. He was a
superb scholar, but pooh-poohed this. 'I am not a scholar,' he

Sutra reading in a temple at Uji

would say. If he were sitting here he would explain that the scholar in his logical, objective thinking sets himself apart from what he is pursuing, hence he always misses the vital point. We must be very careful regarding this process of the awakening experience and bear in mind that it is not just a submersion in the abyss of the unconscious, neither is it a continuation of the conscious state of mind. It is the repossessing of the conscious mind after it has gone through the cosmic unconscious."

I ask, "Is there not a bit too much emphasis on expectation of *satori* in modern Zen, as if enlightenment were something to be forced at all cost? To me Zen's enormous merit really is the awakening and vitalizing of our intuition that one has an abiding option of awakening, of finding the 'kingdom within'—and no where else! Zen keeps alive our trust that notwithstanding all our delusions, the 'kingdom is within'—always available. I, as a member of the human race, am karma accumulated from the birth of this race. At the same time as a human being I am Buddha Nature. The greatest Zen saying to me is perhaps Dogen's, 'All beings *are* the Buddha Nature.' In Christian language one could translate it as 'Every being is a Christophany.' It is the ultimate demand for absolute reverence for every human life in particular."

"What you have said, I could have said. Many young people, American, Japanese, Swedish come here. Mostly they want to talk. They are usually between 20 and 30, and very, very troubled. I ask them, 'Who are you?' I can see it in their eyes if they use drugs."

"I don't think they would come to you unless they have in some way already asked themselves 'Who am I?' Isn't that the question that proves that one is human, the question that shows the first signs of a desire to be liberated from the isolated ego?"

He nods repeatedly.

"What is your attitude towards the so-called mind-expanding drugs?"

"Absolutely against! There are no short-cuts! Self-indulgence never leads to anything worthwhile. It is not enough to see the light.

I have to repeat that to these young Westerners. It is not enough to have insight and freedom. Freedom without self-discipline leads nowhere. We have to learn again how to live together, how to do a task properly, how to get up, how to wash, how to work, how to have respect for others."

While we talk I have started to draw him. "I hope you don't mind," I say. I scribble, hardly looking at my paper. "Drawing is my way of seeing, it is also my spiritual discipline. While drawing, one is for the time being absorbed in the absolute present. One does not 'portray' a thing or a being, one is in immediate experiential contact, 'in touch' with it, one becomes 'it.' "

"What are you in contact with?"

"That is indefinable, can't be expressed except in the act of drawing. Sometimes in drawing a face I have the feeling that I see at the same time the accumulated karma and the Buddha Nature. If not, I know I am drawing a caricature. The difficulty is to screen out all meddlesome thought. Its interference negates the 'being in touch.'"

"It is that way in zazen," he says. "Too much thinking makes one nervous, pointed, sharp like the point of a drop of water instead of the rounded surface of the drop. Not giving in to that temptation to formulate, to conceptualize, that is Zen."

I ask him about Professor Keiji Nishitani, whom I have just discovered in a magazine called *Eastern Buddhist.*

"He is a truly trained philosopher and mathematician but he, too, is much more than a philosopher. He goes beyond words, beyond philosophy. He writes finely crafted sentences that come out of his personally attained insights."

"It does not read like philosophy or theology."

"Both Suzuki and Nishitani were students of Kitaro Nishida, probably our greatest thinker. They are indeed not theologians in the western sense. Theologians are people who dig, find interesting stones to look at, go on digging, unearth more and more fascinating rocks but always stop short of where the groundwater starts. It is the groundwater that matters."

There is a knock. One of Kobori's students announces an urgent telephone call.

"Unnecessary intrusion," Kobori sighs, sitting down on his cushion again. "One just has to obey. That is modern life. But we spoke about groundwater. Where there is no water, there is no health. I am not digging for stones but for water. This is what is going on here all day. It is not 'Buddhism,' not 'Zen,' it is simply digging for the groundwater. I have to fashion a scoop, literally a scoop for each individual to draw the real water. That is my profession. How to communicate? How to cut the green branch of the tree, keeping it green?"

"Isn't that the art of the Bodhisattva?" I ask.

"The Bodhisattva," says Kobori, "is not someone enjoying himself. Neither is he without desire. He is obsessed with one desire, the desire to communicate, to scoop up the groundwater, to offer living water to drink. So the Bodhisattva suffers as Christ suffers. Where the groundwater is reached, after piercing all the layers of meaninglessness, we are all One. The individual spirit, through the experience of its total humanness, is elevated from the level of discrimination and finitude to the level of nondiscrimination and infinity. No longer is it enclosed in a walled-off ego which rejects egos. It stands on the basis of 'being' which everybody and everything equally share, is immersed in the fountainhead of eternal life. At the root of one's individuality lies the universal, infinite human nature. Here all human beings can understand and respect one another. Here begins the awakening of what the Lankavatara Sutra calls the Great Compassionate Heart and the Supreme Wisdom that can be shared by all of humanity. One could also put it"—he interrupted himself with a desperate gesture and mumbling "words, words, words"—"that the sensitivity of the great Wisdom is Compassion."

"May I come back to Daisetz Suzuki, Reverend Kobori? How would you assess his significance for East and West?"

"Suzuki lived in the ebb tide," he said. "He sat in the boat that rode the first great wave of the tide. In the ebb tide all principles that had guided us had lost their authority. We came to assume that 'God is dead.' We began to presume the part of the Creator, finding in our machines something approximating the creative power of the Creator. We believed that science-technology would give us some kind of heaven on earth but by now we are aware that life has become empty, meaningless, and feel in despair how alienated we have become from ourselves and how afraid we are that science/technology may well wipe us from the face of the earth. What Suzuki attempted to introduce is a new standpoint. What he had to contribute, I believe, is the idea of a total person, in whom wisdom and love are deeply rooted and whose love and wisdom will be able to assume control of all scientific and technological know-how to save humankind from self-destruction, a love that, by providing the basic understanding of what is human, will make a basic harmony between humankind and nature possible."

In the noise of traffic and loudspeakers blaring from the election sound trucks, I walk back to the center of Kyoto through streaming rain, surrounded by the signs I can't read, the voices I can't understand, by the raw roar of life. Groundwater. Living water.

At the library Michiko-san, instead of going out for lunch, is waiting for my return. I have to repeat word for word my conversation with Kobori-sensei. She has practiced zazen in one of his groups, and has a profound reverence for him. In her very pragmatic way I find her pervaded with spirituality, that of Buddhism. Her understanding is no less profound than that of the professors.

"The Japanese Christians I meet here," she says, "are mostly ministers. They are very fine people, but I can't help thinking that they have forced themselves into a Christian phraseology that does not come naturally to us Japanese. It is all so abstract and rigid. And in their articles and sermons they talk so much of God, praise him so highly and constantly you'd nearly think they talk about a boss they don't really like. There is always talk about 'God's will, God's plan,' and 'God's purpose,' as if God sat there willing and planning all the time, while keeping them informed by telephone."

"What could the 'will of God' mean to you?"

"The will of God," Michiko says, her little face suddenly turning into the impersonal one of the tea ceremony, "the will of God is the will of the 'True Human-without-status in the mass of naked flesh!'"

Michiko refers here to the story of Rinzai's famous sermon to his monks. Rinzai, the ninth-century Chinese founder of what is still the largest Zen sect in Japan, said to his monks, "There is the True Human-without-status in the mass of naked flesh, who goes in and out from your facial gates (sense organs)." Then he called out, "Those of you who have not yet witnessed to him: Look! Look!"

A monk asked, "Who is this True Human-without-status?"

Rinzai grabbed him by the throat and cried, "Speak! Speak!"

The monk hesitated and Rinzai let go with the words, "What a worthless stick of dirt this Human-without-status still is!"

"If Rinzai were to ask you, you would take out your pen and draw him, wouldn't you?" says Michiko.

It is not the first time Michiko-san gives me a shock. Often she only hints by a word, she has no complex philosophical theories. She has, as a Zen saying puts it, "the woman's mind: I like him because I like him," and she does not misjudge what she likes. When I tell her so she quotes Ikkyu: "As for the skin, how different a man and a woman, but as to the bones they are both human."

The Gōo Jinja, a Shinto shrine, stands opposite the Imperial Palace, behind high walls, hidden by tall trees. Its courtyard is dominated by a life-size sculpture of a wild boar. Behind it on the raised platform of the closed shrine stand barrels of sake, sacrifices to the god enshrined inside.

This Kami or god is, as is often the case, a divinized human being, the medieval hero Wake-no-Kiyomaro, faithful protector of the Imperial House. The wild boar is his intermediary, the messenger between the god and us mortals, in a sense perhaps Wake-no-Kiyomaro's totem animal.

On a radiant Sunday morning in spring the shrine is festively decorated with mauve banners. In the grounds, children are catching goldfish from large flat basins, carrying away their prizes, living mobiles, in clear plastic bags filled with water. A man sells spun sugar on bamboo sticks. Forty little boys in white jujitsu uniforms are being drilled in a corner of the yard by a young man with a black belt. They perform like synchronized mechanical toys. Then, at the end of one series of exercises they run over for spun sugar and offer me a lick. In front of the shrine men and women, in identical brown happycoats over their Sunday clothes, uniform of the congregation, pose for photographs with three small children in glorious red kimonos. An apple-cheeked boy of four wears a gold, foot-high Shinto priest's hat, the girls gold crowns with mobile, springy gold twigs and ornaments, fastened on a tiny scarlet cushion that is tied on their straight black hair. Their little faces are made up in white, with red cheeks and much black eye-shadow.

Suddenly technotronic Japan has disappeared. The center of Kyoto has become a timeless village. On the raised balcony of the shrine two priests, in long white flowing robes and pinched conical foot-high ceremonial hats, performing a liturgy, kneel and bow, agitate green-leafed branches. Meanwhile the jujitsu club performs a demonstration in homage to the god. A little old truck decked out with all too pink plastic cherry blossoms and a hoarse loudspeaker pulls up in front of the gate. The head priest, a hieratic figure, his wisp of white beard in the wind, strides towards the gate, swinging a leafed branch rhythmically in blessing. The procession winds endlessly through the narrow back streets. People watch it pass from their brown wooden houses. At the end of the procession a dozen women carrying plastic bags and pincers, pick up every single scrap of paper,

Shinto Ceremony, Gōō Shrine, Kyoto.

every cigarette butt, every wrapper in the street, as a humble act
of purification.

In the train to Nara, the eighth-century capital, a young woman
in grey suit and miniskirt opens her blouse and suckles her
two-year-old girl from a small, flabby breast. No one takes
notice. At the station Nara seems less an ancient capital than a
replica of a Westchester town with new apartment blocks, lun-
cheonettes, and square office buildings. But within a three-
minute walk the reflection of the 1,600-foot-high five-storied
pagoda of Kofukuji shrine placidly trembles in the Sarusawa
pond, where in the old days people used to set free the fish they
bought from fishmongers, in order to accumulate merit for their
dead relatives.

But I am not in Nara for sightseeing, not even the famous fres-
coes of Horyuji tempt me. My objective is Todaiji, the ancient
headquarters of the tiny Kegon sect, matrix of the climax of
Buddhist thought as it developed in India, China, and Japan.

It would be utterly presumptuous to attempt a glib summary
of Kegon, this exalted apex of human spirituality. Legend has it
that Fa Tsang (643-712), the third patriarch of the school, demonstrated the basic principle of Kegon (or *Hua-yen* in Chinese) to
the Empress of China by setting up mirrors at the eight points of
the compass, at the zenith, and at the nadir. He then placed a
lighted candle at the center. Each of the ten mirrors reflects the
candle. Picking out one particular mirror, it too, of course, is
seen to reflect the candle, but at the same time it picks up the
reflection of the candle in all the other mirrors. Each one of the
nine is in the one, not just individually but totally. If one reflection in one of the mirrors is interfered with, all reflections are
affected, mutilated.

Fa Tsang offers his mirror-parable as merely approximative,
static, a spatial image of what is perceived as taking place in
unimaginable dynamically interrelated complexity in the universe. The parable is akin to the Hindu symbol of Indra's net, a
net that carries a bright precious stone on each knot of its mesh

so that each jewel reflects all the other jewels' brilliance, symbolizing the way in which all phenomena of the relative world are mutually permeating and reflecting.

Kegon is based on the Avatamsaka Sutra and a treasure house of as yet untranslated Chinese literature. The One and the Many, God and his Creation are encompassed in its vision of a united field, directly, experientially perceived, embracing not only the relationship between the One and the Many, between God and each individual existence, but also that between each individual existence and all others as one of mutual interpenetration, unimpeded and total, in which things and beings—while retaining their unique identity—are seen as wholly interdependent and in a sense equivalent, even interchangeable. It embodies a radical ecological insight into the cosmic process which predates our fumblings in this direction by nearly two thousand years.

Emperor Shomu (724-748), its founder, tried in vain to base his government on Kegon principles: the demands it makes on imagination and intellect were too great.

One approaches Todaiji, one of the few remaining Kegon monasteries, by an avenue lined with stalls that sell the Buddhist counterpart of Lourdes-junk, through a vast park where hundreds of deer roam in freedom, fed by the thousands of daily visitors attracted more by the "national treasures" in the Todaiji compound than by its Kegon heritage. The omnivorous and pathetic deer gorge themselves on cookies, rolls, *sushi*, and cellophane bags with undiscriminating voracity. Through an enormous faded pink and sky-blue gate-building with terrifying 25-foot-tall door guardians, the gigantic Daibutsu-Den, the Buddha Hall, is seen rising at the end of a wide avenue, gaunt, ghostly, and grandiose, the largest wooden building in the world—two stories of brown cedar with faded whitewash under a roof crowned with the horn-shaped gilded ornaments called *shibi*, bird tails, charms against fire.

The Vairocana Buddha of Todaji, Nara

In the center of the dimly lit hall, 187 feet wide, 160 feet high, sits the Mahavairocana or Sun-Buddha of Kegon. His body is infinitely great, his life infinitely long. He is the sun that illuminates the darkest corners of the universe and casts no shadow. More than fifty feet high, the Cosmic Buddha sits in tranquillity, one gigantic ten-foot-high hand raised in front of his right shoulder, the other lying open on his left knee. The half-closed eyes stare across limitless horizons. A gigantic lotus flower is his throne. According to the Avatamsaka Sutra the world is created through the vows and practices of this pantocrator, preaching eternally for the salvation of all beings. But people saunter chattering, laughing around the colossal bronze image that dwarfs them, loiter around the luminous Vairocana, call out to their children who hold crawling contests through a hole in one of the enormous pillars at the statue's back. Then they amble out of the sanctuary and back into the sunshine. Who listens to the eternal sermons of salvation?

An ancient wooden figure, stern-faced, dressed in a red cloth cap and cape, enthroned in lotus position at Todaiji's entrance, is treated with more consideration. People rub the ancient wood of Pundola Bharadvaja, the Miraculous Healer, then touch their chests, throats, foreheads.

In the Sangatsu-do or Hokkedo, the simple one-story building, where, in the eighth century, the Kegon sutra was first preached in Japan by a Korean monk, it is quiet at last. A few people sit silently in contemplation of the sublimely tranquil seventh-century Kwannon, who in her mercy heals those who are mentally troubled, leads them to the world of enlightenment with the silk cord hanging from her third left hand. She is flanked by two tender images of white clay, Sunlight and Moonlight, their hands joined in veneration, their faces all but imperceptibly smiling in infinite gentleness. This is holy ground.

One Saturday afternoon Michiko-san brings her friends from Osaka to tea. A secretary, a translator, three students, all speak English. Here as in Europe, in America, it is as if in the young a mutation were taking place, as if from unsuspected depths a wave were rising, a mass movement without cohesion, without center. Their generation, invaded by the noise of radio and television from its first day, brainwashed without pause by the most pervasive commercial and political propaganda, should have been poisoned to its very core. Yet, suddenly, many, many among them show that something inside has hardly been touched, has remained immune to it all. In Japan too they confront their own lives, see their dehumanized future in a computerized society and ask in horror the eternal questions, Why am I here? Who am I? Who are you? What is the meaning of our lives? Where the concentration of poison is greatest, the Spirit seems to manifest itself, where dehumanization is almost complete, the Specifically Human within may assert itself.

"Who in Japan asks these questions, Michiko-san?"

"The Human-without-status asks these questions," she says.

"What is the answer, Michiko-san?"

"The Human-without-status is the answer," she says with a smile that frowns.

Nō drama: Dance

ᛣ *Nō Drama* ᛣ

Twenty minutes by taxi from Kyoto lies the commune of Itto-en, the "Garden of One Light." In a narrow valley, along a rustling brook, in a garden that epitomizes with its miniature bridges, narrow paths, careful plantings, all Japanese gardens, a score of simple buildings houses the 250 members who have given up the world of competitive struggle for life, followers of Tenko Nishida who founded this commune in 1905. He died a number of years ago, in his nineties. Tenko-san was successful as a businessman and agricultural engineer when, still a young man, he suddenly gave up everything. He became voluntarily penniless in order to search for the meaning of life, in total dependence on God, a seeker "seeking first the Kingdom" in the faith that all things shall be added, who had never heard of Christ. He went out to serve people without a thought of remuneration. He chose the dirtiest, lowliest work as his free offering to God. He was considered insane, but someone always gave him something to eat. Eventually, disciples gathered around him and he founded Itto-en, where he and his followers lived a life of nonpossession and performed services without demanding payment. Even now, work detachments from Itto-en go to poor neighborhoods to clean streets, scrub toilets in what they call "humble service." The day at Itto-en starts at 4 A.M. when members join in meditation and in the prayer that they may see the Light of Oneness, may worship the essentials of all religions in the aspiration of bringing all religious truths into one. They pray to live in obedience to the laws of nature and to walk in the paradise of Absolute Being, to return to "Humankind's true home" (Nirvana, the kingdom). The tract of land given to Tenko-san and his community by friends was made into the admirable estate I was guided through by Ayaka Isayama, a tiny woman in her forties with the serene face of a contemplative nun.

"Is Itto-en now self-supporting?" I asked.

"Yes, we are self-supporting. We operate a printing plant, we publish a magazine and books. We have our vegetable gardens and rice fields where we cultivate superior rice seed, three different varieties, that we sell to farmers all over Japan. We also have a construction company which strives to maintain traditionally fine standards of workmanship. We have our own kindergarten, a primary, middle, and high school and, of course, the Suwaraji Gekien Theatrical Company which performs dramas of spiritual significance all over Japan, in cities as well as hamlets."

"Is there a supporting lay movement attached to Itto-en?"

"Yes. Our peace movement is spread all over the country. Our members do 'humble service,' organize cleaning details for latrines. We give seminars and meditation training to groups from industry and business. And we keep the ideals of Tenko-san alive; our meals are no better than that of the humblest worker. In homes that offer us hospitality we render whatever service is at hand. We respect all, are grateful to all. We are neither priests nor laymen, but attempt to perfect our way of living in complete submission to the laws of nature. Rich men, with worries in spite of their wealth, came to Tenko-san begging for relief. Without uttering many words, he seemed to show them the root of their worries, took them off their shoulders. To poor men he showed their spiritual wealth. He never either affirmed nor denied the prevailing world ideologies. Was he the Light himself? Was he mad? All he wanted was to help end struggle, competition, with all the cheating and cruelty involved, to help end war. Like Saint Francis he chose holy poverty. We follow him," says Ayako Ishayama.

In Tenko-san's simple room, kept as it was on the day of his death, hangs the photograph of one of his closest friends, Mahatma Gandhi.

Ayako visited us in America a few years later. She arrived with ten dollars in her pocket, hitchhiked from San Francisco to New York, and earned her keep by cleaning houses along the way. When I pointed out how dangerous that was, she smiled, "Oh, people were so friendly, so helpful."

In the folder that accompanies the admission ticket to the celebrated
rock garden of Ryoanji, the abbot gives these directions for use: "Sit
down quietly and contemplate this garden of sand and stones. . .
Soami, the famous artist who created this garden here expresses his
understanding of Zen enlightenment with great simplicity. . . View
the garden as a group of mountainous islands in a great ocean, or as
mountaintops rising above a sea of clouds."

On the gallery overlooking the fifteen rocks distributed so cunningly
on a raked surface of sand, only 34 by 16 yards, enclosed by a white
mud wall, stand, kneel, or squat forty or fifty picture-takers. New
hordes of camera toters, shutters cocked, led by a little stewardess with
a flag, push energetically to take their turn.

> *"In softly breathing wind*
> *Man reads in the quietness*
> *Scripture without words"*

says the folder. Thirty tourist buses in the parking lot kept their
engines running for instant departure from the Scripture without
words, the softly breathing wind.

This country with thirteen times the population density of the
United States, drives one into a multilayered claustrophobia. It is
impossible to escape from the ever-present pressure of crowds.
From the uninterrupted electronic din of radios and jukeboxes,
from the compulsive jabbering of loudspeakers on every bus,
train, excursion boat, I flee into Nō drama. Weeks before leaving
Japan, I am asking myself how to live without Nō, having
become addicted.

Watching my first Nō drama was a new initiation into theater,
dance, music, and liturgy. Had I ever seen theater before, or
dance? Had music ever shaken me as totally? Neither description
nor photograph can give an idea of the visceral impact of these
plotless plays, these poetic dramatizations of karma, in which the
rewards and punishments of heroic and villainous lives extend
beyond the limits of physical death. They are expressed in forms

that are distilled by seven centuries of tradition to unimaginable density and subtlety. Nō, as a style, succeeds in compressing the limitless into narrowest limits, of saying the unsayable, of making visible the unseeable. Inexpressible grief is expressed with utter poignancy by a hand slowly raised, thumb folded in, to a barely inclined head. An outburst of shattering despair, anxiety, rage, becomes one single piercing sob. A voyage from one province to another, from heaven to hell, is unmistakably expressed in one single dragging step by the masked actor. Every step has infinite weight. The foot is placed squarely on the ground, then the toes are lifted to touch the ground once again, as if to confirm the foot's awareness of having touched earth. Even when the actor runs forward or backward, each fleeing step is composed of these two motions. Nothing is casual. As in a liturgy, the slightest motion is saturated with transcendent meaning.

Nō manifests clearly what modernized liturgy so often lacks; transcendent meaning is made visible, hearable, feelable. The visual impact of the costumes alone, of these magnificent brocades in rare orchestrations of color, pattern, form, challenges one's full capacity of perception. Yet, it is only a single element in an overwhelming totality of epic, choreography, music, mythic liturgy. The ritualized diction comes reverberating from the roots of human existence. The chant of the chorus is obsessive, penetrates one to the marrow. The musical accompaniment by an orchestra limited to one shrill flute and two or three handdrums whips the heart into wild rhythms. The choreography is turned inward; Nō dance is *dhyana*, Zen contemplation, as pure motion. This baffling complexity of elements Nō welds into a oneness of apparent simplicity by a magic that makes a continuum of all perception, that makes the ears see, the eyes hear, the spirit soar towards its home.

Nō is to Kabuki what the B Minor Mass is to "The Merry Widow." To those addicted to the wild race towards oblivion, insensitive to the inner tension of every motion it is excruciatingly boring. There is precise timing in Nō, but no time. Time here touches eternity, feelably. Now/Here.

Nō can actually be seen only in Japan, for it is acted in specially built theaters, on a bare stage constructed according to seven centuries of tradition. The placement of every pillar, of the "bridge" running from the Green Room's curtain to the main stage, the placement of each actor in relation to the elements of the stage, all details are fixed in this tradition.

In Nō, it is the absence of all efforts of spurious originality that reveals the uniqueness of the actor. The Nō mask, worn by the *shite*, the principal actor, never substitutes for naturalistic make-up. It remains mask, simply tied in front of the actor's face, leaving the throat bare. Yet, the masked actor has not put on a disguise. He has, in full awareness, entered into the mask, filling it with his whole being. As I was drawing the ghost of the poetess Komachi in Kayoi Komachi, I noticed by the texture of the bare throat that the splendid *shite* who played the young girl—all female roles are played by men—was well past middle age.

"That main actor, the *shite*, must be at least sixty," I said to Gondo-san, the manager of the Kanze Nō Theater.

"He is celebrating his seventy-fifth year on stage this year. He is eighty-three, the oldest Nō actor of Japan."

Nō actors start their training at six. By the time they are ten, they play children's parts, but also the part of the emperor. Purity and innocence make the child into the ideal symbol of imperial majesty. Besides, the child actor cannot be considered to be in competition with the all-important *shite*, the principal actor. In a play like "Ataka," the metallic child's soprano suddenly soars above the dark virility of the chorus and the crescendo of drums and flute, in studied mechanical diction. The child's eyes are fixed as in a mask. It makes your hair stand on end.

"The future of Nō is bleak," Gondo-san says. "It becomes more and more difficult to train actors. Even in the families that supplied our finest Nō players for five centuries, today's children

want to be part of the new technological world. The young prefer spectator sports, television, Westerns to Nō.

Should Nō be lost, Japan will have lost its soul.

For days on end I sit in Nō theaters, drawing, until without
understanding the words, I grasp the noble spirit of this liturgical art which, spurning all pseudo-originality, all individualistic
idiosyncrasy, makes visible the uniqueness and authenticity at
the core of every life. The artist's choice is ultimately between
willed originality and naked authenticity. Nō is the liturgy of
human authenticity.

"I wonder," I say to Michiko, "where did you get this answer
about 'the True Human-without-status' being the will of God?"

"I often thought about it, " she said, "and suddenly I knew:
This is it!"

"Did you grow up in a very religious atmosphere?"

"No," she says, "on the contrary. My parents have no interest
in religion at all."

"It was the same for me!" I confess. "Maybe we were lucky.
Maybe one does not need religious indoctrination, maybe the
spiritual imagination is stunted rather than stimulated by it."

"Religious education," says Michiko, "might be something
very different from indoctrination. It might simply consist in an
appeal to the sensibility in a child to its own being and to that of
other creatures. Maybe it is only the being-quality of the parent
or the teacher that can make the appeal. I think a man like
Kobori Sensei has that quality and also Shojun Bando. And of
course Professor Nishitani."

"You should talk to King," Professor Doi said repeatedly.
Professor Winston L. King, on a sabbatical from Vanderbilt
University in Nashville, tall, angular, bearded, and in corduroy,
is charming, direct, unaffected. Of course the subject is
Buddhism, on which he has written brilliantly. He comes from a
fundamentalist Christian background.

"On my father's farm daily bible reading and prayer were

never skipped. My wife and I spent two years in Burma and Thailand, studying Theravada. My wife became somewhat of a Buddhist Christian there. She attended a meditation center."

In Thailand he met Thomas Merton, who died there in 1968. His essays on Zen, we agree, are the profoundest writing on Zen by any Westerner. "He was a transparent human being," said King. Then he spoke about the great interest among his students in Oriental religions.

"They have rejected not only the religious establishments, but their entire religious and ethical systems," he said. "The best ones no longer find support in their inherited faiths, whether Protestant, Catholic, or Jewish. To them they now have little to offer but irrelevant, dead or dying concepts, and symbols produced by defunct civilizations which were based on totally different presuppositions from our own scientific-analytical ones. They don't even bother any longer to attack these structures that simply no longer make religious sense, that no longer provide them with a home for their deepest aspirations. All the frantic attempts at a superficial up-dating, at a revamping of 'relevant' meaning in the Judeo-Christian institutions have been failures. To these young people they are part of our impersonal, or worse, our phony-personal public-relations society that thwarts all emotional participation and growth.

"In the Eastern religions they find a religious content that is flexible in terminology, that does not insist on a literal belief in rigidly delineated, precise concepts, is tolerant of heterodox questioning, and allows liberties to be taken with symbols and formulations which do not pretend to be anything but metaphorical. Oriental religious concerns are not intellectual-conceptual but rather existential-visceral. There is no emphasis on the questionable historicity of the Founder's biography. The symbolism is elastic and even where it seems contradictory, the contradictions may supply further meaning."

Reflecting on this, I asked myself, is this all so new? Were not the same factors at work fifty years ago, perhaps a little deeper underground? Had I not rejected then, together with institutional religion, the Catholic symbolism I had so fondly absorbed from the environment? Had not I been so repelled by political manipulations, the theological rationalizations, the accommodations of the hierarchy even with genocide, that I had concluded that institutional Christianity was totally uninhabitable as a home for the Spirit, human or divine! Only after years of immersion in Eastern thought, in Upanishads and sutras, did I begin to rediscover, not so much "Christianity" as the Christ, with an imagination freed to *see* the sacred myths and symbols and holy jargon as man's attempt to find the meaning of self and world. The biographical details of Jesus and of Gautama I now saw as unimportant compared to their incarnations as Christ and the Buddha. It was the fact of this incarnation that was to be taken as important, crucial.

On Shijo Avenue, a mob of some 200 students in red crash helmets, compressed into a monstrously frantic caterpillar, are jogging six abreast behind red flags, holding on to one another's shoulders. While jogging they emit raucous war cries. The column is flanked on either side by nearly as many riot police as there are demonstrators. Weirdly shocking, menacing, this faceless phalanx of jogging helmets, roaring, moving like an enormous beast, disappears into Maruyama Park. Will the monster turn around, attack, run amok? The tail of the caterpillar disappears under the cherry blossoms, the roar becomes less distinct, then stops. The silence is ominous. A quarter of an hour later Shijo is filled with small groups of students, crash helmets under their arms, walking peacefully on the sidewalk, joking, buying cokes, licking ice-cream cones. Japan!

Shojun Bando is a married priest of the Jodo-Shin sect and professor of Buddhist studies at Otani University. He is a slight young man of that sensitive courtesy and gentleness that is so often striking in Japanese Buddhist scholars, who seem able to combine erudition with natural grace, warm unaffectedness, and simplicity.

"The analogies between Jodo-Shin and Christianity are fascinating," he says. "According to Shinran, our twelfth-century
founder, the Supreme Buddha, of whom he speaks as the
Dharmakaya (the Law-Body, or Body of Reality), or as
'Suchness,' is formless. The moment Suchness manifests itself, it
is no longer 'abstract,' formless, and Shinran then speaks of the
Amida Buddha, the Buddha of Infinite Light and of Eternal Life.
In Shinran's teaching, Amida, without losing his absolute nature,
thus becomes part of the phenomenal world, becomes conceiv-
able and accessible to men, as a savior who redeems and liber-
ates persons who call upon him, evoke his name.

"If the Supreme Buddha evokes similarities with what Eckhart
calls the Godhead, with the ineffable, unknowable, then Amida,
in his role of savior, endowed with two natures, reminds one of
Christ. Also what Shinran calls the 'birth in the Pure Land' is a
concept of salvation analogous to the Christian 'dying to Adam,
living in Christ.'"

"Would you say from the Jodo-Shin point of view that Amida
as a savior is a mediator between man and ultimate reality, as
Christ is for traditional Christians?"

Bando nodded, "Yes, in the sense that Amida wants to gather
all men in the Pure Land, the region where man's spiritual principle is liberated from egoism. The Pure Land is somehow analogous to 'the kingdom within.' The spiritual principle which the
Buddha calls the 'unborn, unbecome, unmade, uncompounded'
which is our potentiality for deliverance from the 'born,' from
egoism, is also what Jesus appeals to in man. His kingdom is not
of this world. What he calls 'this world,' what else could it be
than the world of *maya,* of cosmic illusion, of appearances, of
ignorance. To say it differently, *Maya* is the world as it really
exists, but misinterpreted, mutilated through our lack of insight
into its and our own nature. Salvation by faith in Amida, by
faith in Jesus are analogous; both are the effect of grace.
Whatever the conceptual differences, here in the East as in the
West it means an archetypal mode of man's longing for salvation, for deliverance from delusion, from sin or from *avidya,*

'ignorance' in the sense of un-wisdom, lack of insight. For the West this holy wisdom-compassion is incarnate in Christ."

As I struggle back into my shoes Professor Bando shows me one of his treasures, a calligraphy in English by D. T. Suzuki: "Man's extremity is God's opportunity."
    "And vice versa, of course," we say at the same time.

Later in the taxi, I remember Bando's remark that he who has attained enlightenment, who has realized the kingdom within, exudes it, spreads it, without even trying. Conversely, we who have not realized the kingdom just as naturally add to the misery of our fellow creatures.
    Humans according to both Christianity and Buddhism have the capacity of being "redeemed," "liberated," saved by being reborn—through the realization of their spiritual principle—to the perception of reality. Christianity may speak of "overcoming the First Adam," or being born in Christ or perceiving the inner light, while Buddhism may express it as "transcendental insight" (Lap Thong, Tibet) or Prajna-Karuna, but what matters is the affirmation of this Ingredient X which places man face to face with his reality.
    If this spiritual potential, this specifically human nature is not a figment of the imagination, it must, under whatever name, be present beyond all ethnic, religious, cultural boundaries.
    In our technological world this life-affirming principle must be stressed more than ever, for it is the only basis for an incarnational humanism that may offset the multilayered brainwashing to which people are subjected from cradle to grave and restore the lost connection with our inner self in the all-encompassing Structure of Reality, which may or may not be called God.
    Such an incarnational humanism would be in sharp contrast with that naive optimistic humanism which closes its eyes to the indescribable horror deluded, unregenerate humans are capable of, subject as they are to the ego-other split, of what in Christian terms is called the Fall, in Buddhist terms *Avidya*.

On Karasuma Avenue, seen from the bus, a gilded cupola that peaks out between the high office blocks intrigues me. It appears to belong to a small hexagonal temple, the Rokkaku-do. In its courtyard stands a statue of Shinran (1175-1262), founder of the Jodo-Shin sect, which rejects "self-power" (jiriki) and in its Amida pietism affirms Amida's "other power" (tariki). A legend has it that Shinran walked down every night from Mount Hiei and slept here fitfully between periods of meditation.

It is a tiny oasis. Not a hundred yards from Kyoto's main thoroughfare, the noise of buses and trucks seems to trickle through from afar. Under the eaves of the building, in a tiny shrine sits a three-foot-high smiling figure amidst a profusion of paper offerings and petitionary prayers. Flowers have been left in little bamboo vases for Binzura-san, a miracle healer, who specializes in headaches and indigestion. Old men sunning themselves sit on the benches. Pigeons keep landing on the little shrine of smiling Binzura-san, leaving their gastrointestinal samples, presumably to be diagnosed.

In the dark paneled living room behind a country temple in the little village of Nitogawa close to industrial Otsu, Nishimura-sensei, *(sensei,* which may be translated as professor or doctor, means literally, "twice-born") makes tea. He is a research scholar and professor at the Zen Institute of Hanazona Buddhist University in Kyoto. He has held various teaching positions at American colleges, but he is attached to his function as a country priest.

"Are all your parishioners Zen followers?"

His face is rather hard and ambitious, his English brisk, almost querulous.

"Zen ideas are almost inseparable from Japanese life," he says. "My parishioners happen to follow a Zen priest, but whether he is a Zen or a Shinshu or a Tendai priest, it makes little difference to them. They happen to be born in the Zen sect; but they recite the Nembutsu as if they belonged to Jodo-Shin too and they have Shinto weddings in front of the Buddhist temple! I am the priest here, so I am the one supposed to know everything. They come to me with their problems. They invite me to their homes to gain merits for the spirits of their dead, who are wandering in limbo. They are simple people. They have a spirit of faith, but it is not an intellectualized faith. They have no idea of Buddhist philosophy. They have their own kind of religious experience."

"How about *satori?*" I ask.

"Religious experience is not necessarily *satori*. I have my doubts about this preoccupation with enlightenment. Personally I am not interested in officially certified spiritual experiences. I learned the hard way. I spent my boyhood as the son of a country priest. I worked on the land, accompanied my father to funeral services. The 'pure' Buddhism of men like Suzuki, Abe, Nishitani is much too abstract. People do not understand religion on the level of the elite of the Kyoto School! Religion must be rooted in popular life, otherwise it is a philosophy, not a religion." He spoke gruffly, aggressively.

What had I been to Nishimura? What was his defiance?

The Reverend Ryozo Kuwahara, temple priest in Osaka and professor at a women's university, belongs to the Soto Zen sect, founded by Dōgen in the twelfth century. He studied Zen at Eiheiji, Dōgen's monastery, graduated in Philosophy of Religion from Kyoto University, and took courses at Rice University in Houston.

"Religion should be studied from the point of view of human beings, not from that of God," he says. "The truth is in the human being. It is his Buddha Nature. By starting our study from the human being, we can find the ground the religions have in common."

I mention a survey of religious attitudes of students in the Tokyo area. Seventy percent of those questioned reject religion as being something purely subjective. Only 8 percent admit to some interest in, or affiliation with, an established faith. The other 22 percent have a nagging doubt that perhaps there might be something to religion but wonder if it is more than a palliative for the weak, the unambitious who must lean on something,

or perhaps some relic of the past inherited from primitive ances-
tors.

Kuwahara says, "These surveys are very misleading. They
ask questions like, 'Do you believe in God?' 'Do you belong to a
Buddhist or Christian or Shinto church or temple?' All this is
obsolete. We know that the young, except for some political reason, do not identify with religious institutions. There is no point
in asking them, 'Do you believe in God?' Especially here in
Japan, we have thousands of gods, Kami. The only answer one
could expect is, 'Which one?' A better question would be, 'Have
you asked yourself whether your life has some meaning?' Where
the answer is 'no,' we are dealing with infants, and further questions are useless. Where it is 'yes' we have made contact with
homo religiosus and from there we can continue."

Kuwahara is a convinced adherent of Soto Zen, which holds
that zazen is not a means to an end, but an end in itself.

"In Soto-Zazen there is no awareness of an 'I' practicing
zazen," he says. "Wishing for enlightenment, as in Rinzai Zen, is
still based on dualistic thinking. Just to sit quietly in zazen like a
rock or a block of wood is all there is to it! Zazen is not a means
to an end called enlightenment, zazen *is* enlightenment. It is the
Buddha in us who practices zazen. Dōgen made it clear that all
beings do not *have* the Buddha Nature, but that they *are* the
Buddha Nature."

Noh Play Kumasaka: the demon exorcized

⚴ *Stirrings of the Spirit* ⚴

For my audience with Lord Kosho Otani, abbot of the Nishi Honganji Temple, patriarch of the Jodo-Shin sect, a young professor of Buddhist philosophy at Otani University will act as interpreter.

We walk between shops that sell "religious articles," Buddhist and Shinto altars and shrines, rosaries, banners, gilded Buddhas and Bodhisattvas, incense burners and charms. As we enter the Lord Abbot's residence in Nishi Honganji, the professor slips a black kimono over his blue suit and a narrow ceremonial scarf around his neck. He leaves his shoes next to mine and pulls a brown rosary out of his pocket in preparation for our audience.

We wait in an old-fashioned-modern drawing room. Beyond the picture window, in the center of the closely cropped lawn, ladies in kimonos—they *look* hunchbacked, distorted by the large sashes on their backs—are waiting for two elderly men, nearly identical in their stiff business suits, who bring three aluminum garden chairs. A younger man in a black kimono and a priestly scarf enters from stage right, sits on the middle chair. Two of the women flank him, after much bowing. The others arrange themselves stiffly behind. Someone sets up a tripod, fusses with a camera. The priest, his hands on his knees, widens his grin until all his teeth are bare, the others now smile too and for a second, stand at attention.

Then the priest jumps up, making sweeping, courtly gestures towards the building, starts trotting. The little group trots behind him. From next door come subdued voices. On the lawn three aluminum chairs stand surrounded by void, they *are* the Void.

The Lord Abbot, in his sixties, wears a dark kimono. From his hand dangles a rosary. His movements are courtly, aristocratic; long eyelids lie over prominent, lustrous eyes in a mat-ivory face. He is a direct descendant of Shinran, a close relative of Emperor Hirohito and hereditary patriarch of the Jodo-Shin sect.

Shinto ritual, Kameoka, Japan

"There are, of course, huge differences in philosophy, in disciplines in our many Buddhist sects," he says, "but the underlying aim and principle of Buddhism, which is perennial and which they all share, is man's salvation from delusion. As long as one is merely human, it is impossible, according to our faith, to free oneself of one's fundamental ignorance. As soon as we ordinary people become aware of our ordinariness, we realize that the goal of Buddhahood is not within our grasp. At this point of realization we meet the problem of self-power *(jiriki)* and other-power *(tariki)* head on.

"Our founder Shinran adopted his predecessor Honen's invocation of the Nembutsu, of Amida's name, but discouraged the endless repetition Honen had prescribed. One single Nembutsu pronounced in a thought-moment of total collectedness makes us awaken to the full other-power which is Amitabha; this thought instant is not of the devotee's doing but Amitabha's. It is Amitabha, 'the Buddha of Infinite Light,' becoming active in the devotee."

"Do not Zen and Jodo-Shin become identical in that instant, your Lordship?"

He does not answer directly.

"The Buddha," he then says, "Amitabha or Amida, is the Wholly Other. At the same time he is closest to us. There is a total oneness and at the same time a total separation."

It was as a Buddhist echo of Professor Doi's Christian affirmation, "In Christianity even after salvation, God remains God, man remains man."

"Your Lordship, you have doubtlessly followed contemporary developments in religious thought in the West. The image of a God 'out there' is no longer acceptable to many educated Westerners, who are more inclined to think of God as the ultimate reality or as our deepest ground. May I ask, Do you see the wholly other, Amida, out there—I point at the three empty chairs—or do you too see Amida as present in our deepest layers, where he may be confronted?"

There is a silence. He asks the interpreter to translate my question once more into Japanese. Then he says enigmatically, "The situation is different with reference to the nature of God and that of Amida. We must not contradict Scripture."

I must have asked a tactless question.

We drink tea, go on talking very pleasantly. I notice how polite I can be.

"The Abbot would like to have another session with you next week," the young professor says to my utter surprise, as we walk back to his office.

"Why?"

"I imagine it is in connection with your question about Amida being 'out there.' Lord Kosho has to be extremely careful, you see. He is more or less in the position of the pope. What he says is considered as dogma by his faithful. He is not as conservative as he sounds. We younger faculty members are considered by the conservatives to be heretical rebels. But the Abbot gives us a great deal of freedom. He even encourages us to be progressive."

"I find it all very confusing," I begin, "here is the Buddha, the great radical demythologizer. . ."

"Correct," the professor smiles, "and you mean to say the sects remythologize him with a vengeance."

"Exactly!"

"Our Buddhist theologians, like your Christian ones, are obsessed with abstruse ideas. They are both ignorant of, or worse, they are disinterested in, the relative reality of people-in-the-concrete. They fail completely to clarify the position of humans in this world as social and historical beings.'

"Both in Christianity and in Buddhism the function of theologies seems to be to block instead of to stimulate self-confrontation, authentic experience. Theologians devote all their time and ingeniousness to inhuman purposes, to abstract constructs, to hair-splitting. What is inhuman is anti-human! No wonder the young don't want to have anything to do with us anymore! So we claim grandiosely that what we have to contribute is too profound for a superficial age, and we conveniently forget that we harangue them in a kind of jargon that is a thousand years old.

Shinto worship, Oomoto, Ayabe

No doubt, what we have to sell is worthwhile. But the language in which we try to sell it has become unintelligible. You have been outspoken, so let me be outspoken too!"

On my second visit to Lord Kosho Otani I have my sketchbook and draw him during our talk.

"You don't mind, your Lordship?"

"Not at all!"

"Could you refresh my memory on last week's conversation?" he starts with a charming smile.

"*Tariki* and *jiriki*. And the question whether Amida is out-there or in-here."

"Yes, let me come back to your question about Amida. I explained to you that we are too miserable, too defiled as creatures to contribute through self-power to our salvation, that all we can do is to open ourselves up to Amida's grace, as one might express it. Now there is indeed a trend among our younger scholars to believe that Amida is to be found within. Still, according to the continuity of the traditional teaching, I would say that Amida is not *only* in our hearts. But indeed, the tendency now is to look for him there. Wherever he is, he can only be found by those who have an absolute conviction or faith in his other-power."

"What did he say?" Michiko asked, looking up from her card catalog.

"He said, 'Amida Saves.'"

The Hieian shrine is a cold, probably nationalistic Shinto landmark. During the cherry-blossom season tourist buses converge on it from all over Japan. In the spring shower the famous "drooping cherry trees" stand in full bloom, spreading a roof of wet, gleaming pink and white above muddy paths. Across the great pond with its causeway of round, flat stepping stones, a field of purple irises stands singing in the grisaille. In the window of the teahouse a waitress in elaborate geisha hairdo watches the shower.

There will be a performance of traditional dances today. Wet people in raincoats huddle together to see the geishas dance.

Their faces are made up in chalk-white that leaves in the nape of the neck a suggestive triangle of natural skin color. Their eyes stand huge and black in the white masks with the tiny blood-red lips. Their bodies move in a ritualized, mincingly dignified caricature of female seductiveness.

Then follows an ancient shamanistic dance by two Mikos, the "vestal virgins" of the Shinto shrine. It contrasts sharply with the affected grace of the geishas. Both priestesses are in their thirties, dressed in white starched tunics over wide ankle-length scarlet skirts, their black tresses are gathered in a white paper sheath. They wear the tinkling crown-shaped gilded headdress often seen in Nō. Their dance is a stately stylization of inwardness to the solemn music of a huge suspended drum, beaten by a woman whose hand moves in a forward-backward rotation as in a trance of its own. A Shinto priest in his tall straw headdress plays the shrill flute. In the first dance the Mikos weave patterns of space with a bouquet of purple iris, and with a bamboo fan with long tassels.

In the sword dance that follows, swords are unsheathed in extreme slow motion, by hands hidden under the long white sleeves. The veiled hands dance with magic grace, half-seen, half-guessed. For the Mikos the audience does not exist, they perform a liturgy of the invisible, in sheer inwardness.

As at my first Nō play, I see the dance as re-creation of the human form in its ultimate dignity and sacredness.

I did not go to Kamakura to see the famous and gigantic Buddha, but because Daisetz Suzuki lived and wrote until his death in 1966 in Kamakura, the thirteenth-century capital, where with feudal patronage Chinese monks founded Engakuji under Bukko, and brought Zen to Japan. Calligraphy, Zen painting, flower arrangements, Nō drama, all this can be traced to Kamakura.

Foolishly I expected a great monastery, a thirteenth-century city nestled in wooded hills. I find a beach covered with plastic bottles and debris, the flotsam and jetsam of industrial Japan, below heavy acid clouds, and a town that is a sprawling, dull dormitory suburb of

Tokyo, a dusty desert of mean tract houses, workshops, supermarkets, and service stations. Engakuji's grounds are the green annex of a choked parking lot. The monastery's cemetery has become a lovers' lane, where couples find a last oasis of greenery, a last refuge for holding hands. Lovers are sitting on Suzuki's simple grave.

Professor Keiji Nishitani is generally regarded as the dean of Buddhist philosophy. After retiring from Kyoto University, he teaches at Otani University and has been a visiting professor in Syracuse, New York and Hamburg. He is also the editor of the splendid *Eastern Buddhist* magazine, founded in 1921 by Daisetz Suzuki, whose fellow student he was under Kitaro Nishida. One speaks of him with reverence, but he seems unaware of it. When I ask about a magistral paper he wrote a few years ago, he looks imploringly at his assistant translator, Norman Waddell, as if to say, "No idea what he is talking about, maybe you remember."
  He is in his late seventies. His face is extraordinary, Japanese but with a highly sophisticated, almost Semitic, profile that recalls Chagall's. I draw him first at one of his lectures at the Center. His movements are youthful, light. During the question period he drapes himself on his folding chair, relaxed as if at a picnic. He answers quietly with the humane humor that must have molded these features, always on the verge of an indulgent smile. For a Japanese he is extraordinarily informal, relaxed.

I meet him at the NCC Center and congratulate him. He has just received the Goethe Prize, and will leave next week for Germany to accept it. "Why they had to pick on me. . .?" he smiles apologetically.

"When I first read of Sunyata as encompassing Ultimate Reality, beyond being and nonbeing, it was like *déjà vu,* a confirmation, an echo of something that lay waiting within me," I said. "I had a similar sensation of 'recognition' when I first read about *ji-ji-muge hokkai,* Kegon's model of the universe. An intuition of it, however deficient, vague, must have preexisted within me."

Keiji Nishitani

"What is your understanding of Sunyata?" Nishitani asked.

"I realize all too well that it is ludicrous to try to express in a few well-chosen words what cannot be expressed. But if you want me to stammer, or even worse, to quote, 'There is no English equivalent for Sunyata.' Inadequate translations are: 'Emptiness,' 'the void,' 'Nothingness.' I myself prefer 'No-Thingness' or 'the ground of Existence-Nonexistence.' It is neither symbol, nor abstract concept.'

"It is absolute reality, experienced beyond all categories of logic, as what is transcendent-immanent and makes my and your relative reality possible. It is the formless that contains in itself the infinite potentiality that participates integrally in all that is. It is absolute time, absolute space. All that is, is suffused by it, may become the instrument of its realization, which at the same time is the very realization of our own true self. If regarded as a symbol instead of as an experience, it could be called an infinity-symbol, one that encompasses all phenomena of the time-space continuum as being mutually interdependent. Words, words . . . This hand is Sunyata. This voice is Sunyata . . . The word refers in a negative way to what in positive terms is expressed by the word *suchness*."

Nishitani nodded.

"And what does *ji-ji-muge hokkai* mean to you?"

This was obviously a good-humored exam.

"You are not tired of my stammering mixtures of words? This is just as inadequately expressible. It is the universe perceived, experienced as an organic whole in which each individual existence is interdependent with, is reflected by, and interfused with every other form of existence in an infinite, living process of becoming and disappearing, a continuum of no-Thingness yet infinitely differentiated, now/here. The relationships of the one to the many as well as that of the many to one another, are clarified in this view. The riddle is solved. Terms like immanence, transcendence, theism, atheism, pantheism become meaningless."

"Where does your awareness of it fit in?" he questioned me, suddenly curt, unsmiling.

"It is part of it."

"Yes," he said, "the universe is the mirror of your consciousness. Insight comes from the universe. It goes back into the universe. That is the self, beyond consciousness, unattainable."

At the end of the lecture at the Center, a Catholic priest asked him, "What points of contact do you see between Zen and Western thought?"

Nishitani quoted Saint John of the Cross, Eckhart, Boehme. Afterwards he said, "They always ask that question! Could you think of other examples?"

Immediately the childlike rhymes of that underrated seventeenth-century German mystic Angelus Silesius, Johannes Scheffler, sprang to mind:

> "Stop, where doest thou run!
> God's heaven is in thee.
> If thou seekest elsewhere,
> never shall thou see!"

> Nothingness thou art
> bottomless Abyss
> to see Abyss in all that is
> is seeing That Which Is

And:

> "In good time we shall see
> God and his light you say!
> Fool, never shall you see
> what you don't see today!"

"Isn't that Western Zen?" I asked.

He nodded. "Where else do you find it?"

"I meet it all the time in the encounters with the many young people who visit my modest trans-religious—or call it generically religious—sanctuary devoted to peace and sanity which I built in Warwick, 50 miles from New York City. It is a non-church, it does not offer services, nor indoctrination. Through its works of art, its Judeo-Christian and Buddhist symbols, it invites to what one might call free association with the Spirit, with the human center. These young people often say, 'Here I can meet myself. Here I can be at peace,' or they ask the pathetic question, 'Why aren't there more places like this for people like me?'

"I understand these responses as an expression of their need for another kind of life, of their feeling that they ought to know who they are, what this life is about. They realize they are being cheated and confused by the unending stream of words and images that artificially create their needs and desires. What speaks here is their urge towards health in a culture that has fouled its nest, the earth, probably beyond redemption. What strikes me especially in these encounters with the young is the surprising extent to which vaguely Zen-like questionings and ideas, however misunderstood, have percolated through a whole generation. Zen is no longer a chic exotic import. Almost subliminally many of its aspects are becoming absorbed in the inner life of the West, assume an occidental life of their own. The confrontation with Buddhism, with Eastern thought has become a real encounter. That encounter is a subject by itself."

Nishitani said, "There is a Zen story that epitomizes the encounter situation of one man encountering another, of I and Thou. In my view it goes further than Buber's I-and-Thou relationship. Just listen:

"Two Zen sages, Ejaku and Enen meet. Ejaku asks Enen, 'What's your name?'

"Enen replies, 'My name is Ejaku.'

"'C'mon,' says Ejaku, 'Ejaku, that is me!'

"'All right,' says Enen, 'then my name is Enen.'

"Ejaku roars with laughter. And that is the whole story."

"Originally the name of a person stood for its bearer's very being. The invocation of the name of Christ, of Amida, of God, points to this momentous significance of a name. On entering the religious life or after a rite of passage, a new name, and with it a new mode of being, is often assumed.

"Enen and Ejaku's game with names is not just an intellectual game. It is an exploration of reality. By answering with 'Ejaku,' Enen steals, as it were, Ejaku's 'being,' his ego. Here the 'I' is no longer standing in absolute opposition to the 'Thou.' It is no longer a matter of 'I' versus 'Thou.' The 'I' becomes the 'Thou.' And yet at the same time each 'I' remains a true 'I,' a genuine subject, absolutely differentiated from the other. But it is a differentiation on the ground of absolute nondifferentiation, for both are rooted in that absolute identity where *I am* Thou, and vice versa. Enen becomes 'other-centric' instead of 'ego-centric' when he calls himself Ejaku. He empties himself of his obsession with having an absolute ego. Absolute opposition becomes absolute harmony, love. Self and other are not one, and not two. In their presumed subjectivity I and Thou are absolutes. In the reality of their relatedness they become absolutely relative. The little self of each dissolves. This is the ground, the bottom of the I-Thou encounter. Unless it is reached and pierced between persons, nations, there remains the struggle of wild wolves.

"The ego-obsession that is conquered in this story is rooted in the Primal Ignorance *(avidya)*, the profound blindness at the root of human intellect, where illusions and suffering have their source. Where the plane of duality, of self versus not-self is transcended, the light of Mahaprajna (Supreme Insight) breaks up this ignorance and the Supreme Compassion is born (Mahakaruna).

"It goes without saying that this cannot be achieved by a purely intellectual affirmation of nonduality, for that would be no more than a displacement of one obsession, one attachment, by another. It can only be achieved by a breakthrough, a *turn-about*, a penetration into reality. The roar of laughter is the essence of the whole fable. It is," Nishitani ended, "like the ancient battlefield the poet Bashō speaks of:

      'Ah, summer grasses!
      All that remains of the warrior's dreams!'"

Nishitani sees as the root conflict of our time that between myth and science, which started in the Renaissance with the shift from the medieval, mythic-religious orientation to the scientific worldview on which modern society was founded and which finally brought it close to total dehumanization. This eighteenth and nineteenth century science and the scientism derived from it, saw the world, inclusive interpersonal relationships as being purely mechanical. It was totally alienated from the depth dimensions of Being. It was in conflict with myth and religion as such, and resulted in the dominance over our society by a multitude of forms of modern nihilism. In our century science is undergoing highly positive mutations, but technology and business are still mired in the anti-human mentality of "classical," this is obsolete, scientism. We cannot go home again to the mythical worldview and ever since Plato and Aristotle actually, a resynthesis of myth and *logos* has been attempted in vain.

    The consciousness of the scientist, in his mechanized, dead and dumb universe, logically reaches the point where—if he practices his science existentially and not merely intellectually—the meaning of his own existence becomes an absurdity and he stands on the rim of the abyss of *nihil*, face to face with his own nothingness. People are not aware of this dilemma. That it does not cause great concern is in itself a symptom of the submarine earthquake of which our most desperate world-problems are merely symptomatic.

    The impasse, contained in the scientific viewpoint itself, can only be broken through by the attainment of a view of nothingness which goes further than, which transcends, the *nihil* of nihilism. The basic Buddhist insight of Sunyata, usually translated as "emptiness," "the void," or "no-Thingness" that transcends this *nihil*, offers a viewpoint that has no equivalent in Western thought.

According to Nishitani, the "individual" as ego, was in the West undiscovered until the beginning of the modern era. From medieval God-centeredness we jumped to an ego-centeredness which in the West was not analyzed for centuries, as Buddhism and Adaita Vedanta had analyzed it two thousand years ago. In Western civilization some inkling of the equality of humans before God survived, but the essential roots of our humanness were cut and we became hopelessly imprisoned in our newly hypertrophic ego.

All the revolutionary movements in the West were based on ego-affirmation. The until now exploited, humiliated ego must in turn exploit and humiliate its former oppressors. The ancient Buddhist discovery of the identity between self and other, between self and Sunyata, Nishitani sees as the truly revolutionary truth about the human being within us.

Still, in the West, John Scotus Erigena knew, "Each creature is a theophany of Nothingness."

Michiko looks worried. Then she starts, "You remember when you asked me the other day and I answered that it is 'the True Human-Being-without-status' who asks the fundamental questions? Doesn't it mean that the answer to questions like 'Who am I?' can never be expressed in words? The true answer is perhaps nothing more than the *awareness of having the capacity to ask this question* and it is this capacity that reveals my humanness. That is who 'The True Human Being' really is. But how does one get to that point of awareness?"

"I should ask you, for you got there!" I said.

Michiko frown-smiles, "I got nowhere."

"You just said 'nowhere.' Rather say, 'now/here!' You remind me of the monk who asks Gensho, 'Where does one enter on the path of Truth?'

"They were walking along a stream. 'Do you hear the murmuring of the water?' Gensho asked.

"The monk nods.

" 'Well, there does one enter,' says Gensho."

"When I hear you talk about Buddha and Christ, Franck-san, I can't make up my mind whether you are a Christian or a Buddhist. The Christians I talk to at the library are mostly missionaries or ministers and they seem to take Christ very literally as a god or at least as a man who lived two thousand years ago and of whom they "know" all the details. So what are you, Buddhist or Christian? Or both?"

"Sorry, I don't put a label on myself, Michiko. It's up to you! You see, the biographical details of the life of Jusus—unreliable and fragmentary at best—are relatively unimportant to me, as are those of the Buddha. It is the Christ-principle and the Buddha-principle they embody in pure unadulterated form, that I find of the most crucial importance, our Human reality as human beings. I don't doubt the immense differences between the religions, they are—conceptually speaking—incompatible. But I refuse to be drawn into these incompatibilities, for they fuse in the heart.

"I find it absurd to take the gospels literally. They are not gospels of love, contaminated as they are by their authors' prejudices, inciting to projection, fault-finding, hatred, so that they could be used as pretext for unlimited cruelty and persecution. I am as skeptical about many anecdotes surrounding Gautama Buddha, even though Buddhist scripture is innocent of being misused to justify inquisitions and pogroms. But yet I have absolute faith in the Christ-principle and the Buddha-principle— call them analogous, call them equivalent!—in every human being, as his deepest meaning and reality, however deeply buried under ignorance, greed, and cruelty. To follow the Christ, the Buddha, is to follow no one at all. It is the breaking-through to the rock bottom where the question 'Who am I?' wells up. Christ's cry, Abba! Father! is its echo. All action changes!

"Both the Christ and the Buddha are still preaching man's liberation from delusions whether from the Mount or from the Vulture Peak. The trouble is nobody listens."

"Somebody listens," said Michiko.

"Who?"

"The True Human-without-status again!" says Michiko.

"The True Human-without-status is the one who preaches!" I object.

"Don't kid me! We are saying the same thing!"

She laughed—for the first time without a frown.

Masao Abe is a somewhat younger member of the "Kyoto School," but quite typical of these professors without pedantry, saved from sheer intellectualism by years of meditation under Soto, Jodo-Shin, or Zen masters.

Abe contributes the deceptively simple but profound observation that what distinguishes Buddhism fundamentally from Christianity is its profound realization of that universal transitoriness, the process of generation-extinction, of birth-death, appearance and disappearance, which we have in common with all other beings, living and even nonliving, but which only we humans can be aware of. "Buddhist salvation," says Abe, is "the existential realization of the cosmic transciency of all things (ego included), which constitutes seeing the universe 'such as it really is.'" *This realization of transitoriness itself is the so-called Buddha Nature, is Wisdom-Compassion.*

"We do not have 'an awakening,' we humans *are* the very process of awakening." Awakening to what? "To the self-awareness of Sunyata in us, to the cosmic process becoming self-aware in us, through us," he says.

Abe, too, diagnoses an all-pervading nihilism in our society, in which "the supersensual world has lost all its power," a post-Nietzschean nihilism, "beyond religion," against which the traditional religions are powerless. The forces that have banded together to eradicate not only the religious institutions, but—and this is immensely more important—the religious attitude to existence-as-such, replacing it with the counter-myths of facism, marxism, nazism, ethnocentrism. The seriousness of the situation is enormously complicated by factors like urbanization, industrialization, nationalism, commercialism, propaganda, and the population explosion. This postreligious nihilism replaces all values by the Will to Power.

One wonders: Where the Will to Power proves itself so clearly to be counterproductive, forever accelerating the catastrophic insanity of our society, its violence, its dehumanization, its suicidal spoilage of the earth, could not now/here, chastised by pain, *in extremis,* a Will to Meaning arise? And once this Will to Meaning stirs in the depths and we face the human reality in the desert of our insane know-how, may not sanity, wisdom, insight be regained? And what is wisdom if not a radical realism about our human condition, our specifically human destiny, the realization of what it means to be born and to die *as human beings*? From the criteria of the specifically human, and only from these criteria, can the values be derived that are adequate to our survival, to the problems of violence, hunger, and war and the structural changes needed to make the earth habitable again.

There are faint signs of hope that such a Will to Meaning is stirring deep below the surface of the streamlined violence, of the nihilistic chaos that is engulfing us. From the intense appeal of Oriental spirituality, of Hinduist, Buddhist, Taoist worldviews—especially among the intellectual young—one might take a hint about the direction in which such a search for meaning is moving. What makes such ancient Eastern ideas, of Zen for instance—which is still with us decades after the Zen fad has worn off—so timely, so irresistible now, in our world? Could it be Zen's pragmatic directness? Its discounting of speculative metaphysics? Its distrust of language in a society where language has become terminally perverted by ever improved techniques of commercial, ideological, and political lying? Is it perhaps Zen's sane claim to point directly at our innermost nature, at our Original Face, at the fundamental Humanness at the core of our species? Or possibly Zen's declaration of independence from scriptures and external authorities? Its rejection of all sociological, philosophical, sexual labeling and conceptualization? Its radical *diesseitigkeit,* secularity, its concern with the now/here, in a world where all utopian ideologies are discredited and the traditional imagery of an afterlife for the ego has lost all credibility? Or all these factors combined? The conventional goals of progress,

odhidharma scroll in a monastery

wealth, power, luxury, of conspicuous consumption, of keeping up with the Joneses, have lost their axiomatic priority. New ideals, new priorities are being proposed: creativity, self-actualization, and authenticity. Where questions like self-actualization and authenticity are pondered, a further wondering about this self that demands to be actualized becomes inescapable! What is the relationship between self and non-self? What are the limits to the assertion of one's own limited self? What is the human community but a community of selves?

Who is this self? Who am I?

These signs of a new stirring of the Spirit may be disparaged as quietism by activists, as pseudospirituality by the pillars of mainstream tradition, as mysticism by all and sundry who have so long misused this word that a moratorium on its use is overdue.

Instead, one might see in these signs the longing and the search for—even the birth of—a new realism about our human predicament, encompassing the rediscovery of criteria of what is centrally, Specifically Human and of what is less than that.

Such a radical realism, born from pain and despair, would be the very antithesis of that deadly protohuman "realism," that is none other than nihilism—on which what is called *Realpolitik is* based.

After its last three-quarters of a century, this *Realpolitik* with its institutionalized genocide, its regression to terror and torture as means of governance, its insane waste of the substance of the earth and the desecration of all life on its surface, stands convicted as anti-human, anti-life, as ultimately unrealistic, indeed as surrealistically absurd.

It is the *Realpolitik* of delusion, forever condemned to produce the opposite of the goals it pursues, forever sentenced to create the pseudosecurity of Thousand-Year-Reichs, the conceits of Manifest Destiny, soap bubbles that explode into pyramids of corpses.

Yes, any course of action that runs counter to the Will of God— which is the will of the "True-Human-without-status," to the "Light that lightens every person come into the world," to the "true self" of humankind—is doomed in advance!

Of that of which we cannot speak . . . let us by all means stammer, stutter, gesture!

Once more I walk, naked in my clothes, on Karasuma Avenue, where the trees stand in bloom in the chilly evening light. I am a leaf on the tree rooted in no-Thingness; one of these countless leaves, soon to fall off with the others, a leaf fully aware of being leaf instead of tree, aware of the tree that bears me, of the abyss from where the sap rises into the roots that nourished me, made me grow into leafhood, still sustains me.

Leaf I am, fully real, realest reality, be it a provisional, relative reality . . . temporary mask of the void . . . the void in which all is timeless, yet, provisional, a person, a persona, impermanent, fleeting.

John XXIII, Albert Schweitzer, Daisetz Suzuki, the Dalai Lama, Keiji Nishitani, Nanrei Kabori, other fellow-leaves I was allowed to touch in this timeless moment of grace, were transmitters of the message I decoded as pure affirmation, as a hymn to the truly Human life.

Our tree, the Tree of Life, has glorious foliage.

I am neither I nor other. You are neither other nor I. To enact this being not-I-nor-other, this being both-I-and-other, is the partaking of the one Flesh and the one Blood we have been from the beginning, in the most literal sense . . . Living awareness of both the Oneness and Manyness of reality . . . Universal Eucharist . . . If as written words, this is nonsense, let it whisper in the marrow.

A man, colorless, ashen, lets out his mongrel in the falling dusk. His cigarette dangles from hollow cheeks. I have known this man from childhood, have known his dog. A flight of pigeons falls across a black roof. I have known these pigeons forever. Maastricht? Warwick? Kyoto? Home is Now/Here.

Part Two

⚖ Road Signs Along the Way ⚖

The Original Face of Holland

⚱ *Putting Oneself on the Line* ⚱

*The religions become more vital when they send their
roots down below the intellectual surface to the
subconscious depths of Human Nature.*

ARNOLD TOYNBEE

A Zen saying warns: "Don't show your poems to a non-poet."
Still, in what follows, this is the risk I must take, in trust that my
inner process is the Human inner process, as it must be that of
each one of my contemporaries.

Philosophers and theologians have been of little help to me on
my safari through life. They are the intellectuals who pit artists,
seers, mystics, poets one against the other in order to play arbiter
over them.

   The poets, mystics, seers and artists are the ones who took the
risk to "show their poem," to witness to their visions, their pain,
their ecstasy, the ones who put themselves on the line, and so, in
fear and trembling, do I.

   To me too, images, things seen take precedence over intellectual concepts. Glimpses of answers to the riddles of existence
are received in symbols, in poetic and visual imagery, in the
constellations of the sounds, the silences of music. Lacking the
ability to sit down and switch on the thinking machine in the
head, I often wonder whether anyone does, except those virtu-
osi of the intellect with whom I have so little in common. Their
thoughts can be contradicted, their theories debated, their
hypotheses criticized.

   Experiences, things seen, can not, so that in what follows, what
might pass for "thought," has come up uncalled for, as the honey,
or the vinegar, sucked out of pure seeing, of sheer experiencing.

All I know seems to come out of this seeing what I have seen and
therefore I must insert some drawings. Without them I would not
recognize this book as one of mine!

Almost all I have written since I returned from my Asian "pilgrimage to nowhere—to now/here"—dealt in some way or other with seeing the world around us versus mere looking-at it. *The Zen of Seeing, Zen Seeing/Zen Drawing: Meditation in Action, Life Drawing Life* are three of these books in which drawing is described as a remarkable catalyst, an irreplaceable intensifier of perception. I found that the seeing and the drawing may fuse into that single, undivided act I christened "seeing/drawing."

Seeing/drawing becomes a profound mode of meditation, for while practicing it the total concentration is on the tree, the human face you draw. The hand seems to be propelled by a reflex arc that runs from eye to hand. The thinking ego is minimally involved. To *see* is to see the Sacred, to *look-at* the world around you is to miss it!

Thousands of drawings happened since I returned from my Oriental pilgrimage, that brief intermezzo inside the longer—yet all too short—pilgrimage from first cry to last gasp that constitutes a human life.

On this pilgrimage I became—almost half a century ago— deeply involved in Zen. It was an unorthodox Zen, for I did not spend long hours sitting in silent meditation. On the contrary, my heterodox meditation, my zazen, consists in seeing/drawing landscapes, human bodies, cityscapes, trees, mountains.

It is well known that the two surviving schools of Zen are Soto Zen, in which the emphasis is on *shikantaza*, sitting in silent meditation, and Rinzai Zen, of which the central discipline is that of solving the koan, that riddle which, as I hope to clarify, is more than just a riddle.

In my heretical Zen discipline—it was approved of as being the natural one for an artist like me, by the Zen master in Kyoto whom I revere as my mentor—my koan is the face, the human body, the street scene I am drawing.

In order to solve a koan, it is said, one has to become radically identified with it: one has "to become" one's koan.

This is precisely what happens when the seeing and the drawing fuse into seeing/drawing. I do *become* that cloud over the landscape, I *become* those people on the street corner. I am solving the koan of the eye.

That koan runs through one's whole being, as the image of this old Chinese woman ran from eye to hand to precipitate itself on the paper. Yes, I literally *became* this old woman as she became an integral part of me, she had become my koan.

So what is a koan?

D.T. Suzuki (1869-1965) wrote: "The koan is in ourselves and what the Zen Master really does is no more than to point it out, so that we may see it more plainly than before. Each one of us brings it into the world and tries to decipher it before passing away. The koan cuts through all conceits and rationalizations, makes it impossible to evade the ultimate, existential questions by means of intellectual stratagems. It lets the intellect struggle with the solutions it can not reach, until it has to give up when one crutch after the other has been kicked away. Then, in extremis, becoming one with the koan, one may break through the illusions and fictions that fill the mind, and confront, experience, reality 'such as it is. . .'"

The koan is therefore more than the jolting question, the riddle, the conundrum, traditionally formulated in words by the Master, and given to his disciple to digest, in order to test by his answers the measure and authenticity of the insight the student claims to have attained. I feel that for the artists of the Sung Dynasty in China their great ink drawings were not intended or manufactured as "art objects," to be exhibited, but were attempts at solving the koan of the eye. While drawing those evanescent landscapes with tiny figures, they were face to face with Reality. The intellect, the interpretive machinery of the brain, was in freewheel.

Daisetz Teitaro Suzuki

When you take a snapshot, your eye may indeed be *seeing*. Nevertheless the image that looms up in the developer is the product of a chemical process. You only pushed the button! Those Chinese masters knew that in order to solve a koan you have to become it. Unless you become what you draw, you can't draw it. The image has to go through every cell of your body before it reaches the hand that draws! What happens is not only in contrast with the photographic process, it is its precise opposite as it is that of all philosophizing, theologizing, psychologizing about trees, faces, beggars and bullocks.

> "Who is the Buddha?" the monk asked.
> "Mind is the Buddha," the Master answered.
> "Why do you say that mind is the Buddha?"
> "To stop the baby crying!"
> "And when it has stopped crying?"
> "Neither mind nor Buddha," smiled the Master.

The exchange might also have gone quite differently:

> "Who is the Buddha?" the monk asked.
> The Master took his writing brush and drew a pumpkin.
> "You mean to say this pumpkin is the Buddha?"
> The Master took his brush again and drew a gourd, then a crow, a landscape, a face.
> "Well. . . ?" the Master inquired.
> The student stood dumbfounded.
> The Master pushed him out of the door: "See you later!"
> "When?" the student asked.
> The Master slammed the door in his face.

A koan cannot be explained! You catch it, as you catch a joke, or you don't.

The most august sayings of Western scripture are just as impenetrable to common sense, to discursive thinking, to the calculating, speculating intellect. They too are koans, no less jolting, no less enigmatic:

"I am the Way, the Truth and the Life. . ."
"I and My Father are one. . ."
"Before Abraham was I am. . ."
"Who has seen Me, has seen the Father. . ."
"I am the Resurrection and the Life. . ."

To solve these is to solve the Mystery of human existence, "at the point where all metaphysical speculation stops" (Lama Govinda).

Even more jolting it may be to realize that the Man who spoke those koans was himself the Supreme Koan incarnate. Western culture inextricably interwoven with his name, has not only failed to solve this Supreme koan, it failed to recognize it as such.

Our sadly inhuman history is the result, as may become somewhat clarified in what follows.

homeground

Unfathomable Grace,
⚓ Immeasurable Curse ⚓

I was born on the spot and at the moment that the distant rumblings of the typhoon of violence that is still raging were becoming audible. I was five years old, when on August 4, 1914, World War I exploded less than a mile from our house that stood on neutral Dutch ground, just across the Belgian border.

Under a murky red sky the town of Visé was burning. The air was atremble with the booming of the Big Bertha field guns.

On that fateful August day and on this very spot the twentieth century, and with it my life, had started in earnest.

By the time I entered first grade, I had seen horrifying things. Streams of maimed, bleeding human beings on pushcarts and improvised ambulances were trekking across the placid river Meuse, through the soft green hills, into our town.

Endless files of refugees passed my window, carrying their children and a few belongings on their backs. I still see the limping old man whose eye I caught. He carried nothing but his canary in its cage. Hundreds of people were camping in and around the former Dominican Church where I helped carry the pots of thick pea soup my mother cooked for them.

I still see the funny little biplane circling over the roofs, the pilot in his open cockpit in brown leather cap and goggles. By mistake he dropped one of his bombs—it didn't explode—on our neutral playground.

During four long years face to face with all this misery, no one could foresee that we were only living the overture of this century of chaos, unheard-of cruelty, and suffering. These refugees from across the border would be the spearhead of those millions of dispossessed, bereaved, uprooted humans who are still fleeing what was once their home, trudging from frontier to frontier, praying, scheming, to dodge the border guards. For ever since that 4th of August, the horrors of war, famine, revolution, holocaust and genocide have followed one another without let up.

The cruelest superstitions and barbarities of ages past pale next to the new terrors this demented century invented, the primitive atrocities it updated, the unbroken chain of beastliness and ferocity it perpetrated upon human beings, all in this one lifetime. The bloody heresies of our new Dark Ages were in the end to degrade men, women, babes in arms, by nature so fragile and so mortal, to the condition of expendable, disposable things, pieces of used Kleenex. The witchcraft of a technology gone berserk was to transgress against the bounties of earth built up over billions of years, to squander and desecrate them in a few decades.

To have been born on this particular spot was both unfathomable grace and immeasurable curse. To have lived those early years in comparative safety, warmly clothed, well nourished, but in the inescapable presence of suffering and death, sensitized the mind of the child to the mysteries of the human condition, compelled the heart to either open itself to compassion and pain or to shut itself off forever in callousness.

It did more, for the child's questioning found no answer. The grown-ups were preoccupied with rationing coupons, prices of provisions on the black market, offensives, news of advances and retreats, alternating victories and defeats. They had no time to be overly concerned with the impenetrable riddle of what could have unleashed such nightmares of frightfulness.

Neither did they see how in the midst of all this phantasmagoric terror, there were other mysteries, almost as unbearable in their supernal beauty: the pink blossoming of a little apple tree in the backyard, the earthy fragrance of a field of brussels sprouts, the tender little yellow hearts in the white flowers of potato plants, flights of pigeons circling in the sunlight, a million starlings falling out of the clouds to land in half-bare trees where you filled your pockets with the satiny brown chestnuts you would keep forever—all this ecstatic delight in the beauty of the world, all the overwhelming bliss of being alive.

"The spiritual," says Daisetz T. Suzuki, "is pain raised beyond sheer sensation . . ." Where peak experience and abyss experience, overwhelming beauty and inexplicable horror, come together and fuse, they give one a first initiation into the Zen experience.

Could peak experiences and abyss experiences in rapid alternation be all the Zen training one really needs? Could this be what in our time opened the tortured heart of the West to Zen?

Meanwhile, I grew up on our little agnostic-humanistic family island surrounded by the vast Catholic ocean of southern Holland. Not having inherited the agnostic temperament, I absorbed, as by osmosis, the ubiquitous symbols of the surrounding Catholic culture as the only available hooks on which to hang my first intimations of Meaning.

Maastricht, the Trajectum ad Mosam—"ford over the Meuse"—of the Romans, was then still thoroughly under the thumb of an omnipotent cabal of reliably Catholic politicians, devout merchants, God-fearing beer brewers and monsignori. But underground something more basic, more ancestral, still warmly vital, an earthy, almost animistic and Neolithic religiosity had survived. It was less concerned with dogma and doctrine than with things more archetypal: an openness to those virtual, undefinable but sacred Presences that transcend the platitudes of everyday life, to those intuitions of Meaning which may well be the original, the primal religious impulse.

Cast iron crucifixes and sky-blue madonnas stood on every crossroad, bedecked with artificial flowers that around Easter time made place for a profusion of jam jars full of buttercups, daffodils and violets. Through our neutral streets there was a constant trudging of feet on pilgrimage to the shrines of miraculous virgins, saints, even sacred springs.

I remember it now as a kind of Catholic Shinto, for Shinto has a similar capacity for non-theological, direct perception of the sacred. It makes up for a minimum of theological acumen by an intense participation in chants, litanies, processions and rituals. These encompass that entire range of choreographies of awe and piety: that bending of knees and spines, folding of hands, casting

Flanders, rain

down of eyelids, droning of prayers and litanies, that is so universal, so trans-cultural, that it must be part of the genetic coding of our human species.

Like every child I pondered the fundamental riddles that stamp us as human before even entering first grade: Why did my beloved pet die? Where is he now? What is it to die? Who is that God they are talking about?

These perennial questions were exacerbated to a particular urgency watching the uninterrupted stream of refugees, bleeding, dying soldiers, pouring across the border into our neutral Holland. The sudden death of my little bantam rooster, the ever present wounded on their pushcarts, somehow linked themselves with the riddlesome life-size naked man who hung bleeding, dying, on his cross on the wall of the cathedral. I passed him by every day on my way to school.

My schoolmates seemed to take this Jesus in their stride as part of the cityscape. They apparently knew precisely what it took to handle him. To me he was a disquieting enigma. Who was this Christ? Why was he killed? Who killed him? "The Jews," they said. I confronted Emily and Henriette, my white-haired maiden aunts who were more or less Jewish, with the accusation. With a wan smile they spread their hands, pleaded not-guilty, and changed the subject.

The poor wretch on his cross looked harmless enough. He must have been the victim of some vile, cruel error, or perhaps of a murderous infection. There was a roadside shrine close by, devoted to St. Roch, pre-Pasteur specialist in rabies. Had perhaps a kind of rabies caused this war, and all those lacerated dying men on pushcarts? The one on the cross too had been killed, but he, they were adamant, had managed to rise from his grave after just three days.

On Easter Sunday, with all the church bells clanging, the women celebrated his rising by putting on new Easter hats, adorned with life-like roses and bunches of cherries that glistened in the

Crossroad

sun, to watch the wondrous procession that trekked through town. Golden reliquaries of sainted bishops were carried by four-somes of strong youngsters, preceded by fat notables in top hats. The Chief of Police in gala uniform headed the procession, martially perched on placid Troky, the old black gelding rented from the riding stable for the occasion. Uniformed brass bands blew solemn processional oompahs, behind velvet banners on which saints were stitched in gold. A host of angels with organdie wings strewed petals before the portly bishop. In miter and vestments stiff with gold embroidery, he shuffled under a gilded canopy carrying the Most Holy in its radiant monstrance.

By far the most heavenly of the angelic host was blue-eyed Maria, our grocer's daughter. After she had relinquished her wings, she whispered what was already obvious, that indeed today the Saviour had risen. I wondered aloud, however, what precisely the Saviour saves one from. "From hell, from sin!" Maria asserted. Still, I kept puzzling: "What hell, what sin?"

Could it be that hell of terrible killing going on across the border, that stupid sin of always forgetting that however many you kill, you and everybody else has to die anyway sooner or later, like my rooster, like Ann the consumptive blond girl in fourth grade?

During lone boyhood hikes I pondered the fundamental riddles. Sometimes I jotted down provisional solutions. "Who is God?" was answered with "God must be the algebraic sum of all possibilities and impossibilities." I was rather proud of that one, for we had just started algebra. I also solved the problem of sin: "Sins are those silly stupid acts that always miss their target." I was less successful with "What could be worse, more cruel, to have five sardines killed for lunch, or two matjes herrings, or one slice of a big cod?" This was my first, homemade, koan and I tried and tried in vain to solve it. I must have been a slow learner and too fond of herring for it was not until many years later that I found the solution: I became a vegetarian.

I decided that one's soul was "in unbroken contact with God, however we try to forget it." About trees I observed "If you are

in a Flemish village

made to live in a place where there is not a single tree to look at,
you are condemned to go crazy."

My schoolmates did not seem unduly preoccupied with such
problems. They learned their catechism and their laundry lists
of sins by rote, went to confession to be absolved from the
accumulated guilt of which pale, heavy-set nuns kept stoking
up the fires.

Their catechism supplied the answers to most of those questions one dared to ask; discalced Capuchins with coffee-brown
habits and dirty toes, filled in whatever was still unclear.

A Dominican monk in his black and white habit waggled—an
obese penguin—over our playground distributing little tracts with
acid blue pictures of the Virgin. He favored me with his wry grin,
but not with a pamphlet. It was the price I had to pay for being
free as a bird from indoctrination and tiresome Sunday duty.

And so the ever present symbols of the Sacred were free to whisper their profound messages, their mysteries, undistorted by discalced commentators, straight into the heart to be decoded. The
beflowered crucifixes and pale blue madonnas on the crossroads
made the hillsides resound with Glorias in Excelsis.

I had discovered the Prologue to St. John's gospel in the little
black leatherette New Testament that sweet old Mrs. Van 0. had
surreptitiously pressed on me in the hope of saving my heathen
soul. I took the little book out from behind the school books
where I had hidden it and read it again and again until I knew it
by heart. It seemed to contain the solution not only to the riddle
of the man on the cross but of that of my own life. For He, the
crucified one, the Prologue said, was "the Light that all the darkness could not overcome." The crucial point, however, came next:
he was also the Light that lightens *everyone come into the world* as
a human being. It said so emphatically, consequently it included
me! Hadn't I come into the world as a human being? It was reas-
suring, and yet not all too surprising.

This Light had to be what lit your eye the very moment you really *saw* a thing, not in relation to yourself, but as it was in itself! Three-dimensionally! It made you see the majestic poplar in the park not as a thing "out there," as some flat snapshot, but as that unique living, lovable being, brimful of life, rooted in the earth as I was rooted in the earth.

In Dutch we have three words for visual perception; not only is there "seeing," as opposed to mere "looking-at," but also— untranslatable, *schouwen* which is an almost stereoscopic perception, at least three-dimensional, but perhaps even four- dimensional, for in *schouwen* the dimension of time, of the ephemeral and the eternal are included, yes, in my poplar tree. . .

The Light that lightens everyone born human, as the Prologue said it so clearly, was not confined to the man on the cross. However pure in form it must be in him, it was also the very core of one's own nature. Who am I? I am not just Little Me, I am That. What a discovery!

The man on the cross was not a fetish! He was—or maybe he wasn't—God's *only* Son. Still, he stood for the Light that is hid- den in everyone, he was the mirror image of who you *really* were, and vice versa.

It would take a lifetime to ponder it further, but St. John's Prologue would remain the alpha and omega of my own primi- tive Christology—from the wrong side of the tracks. It and the confrontation at Emmaus were the gospel's perimeters, all the rest seemed secondary.

That Light of St. John's Prologue was the core of being human. . .

Years later I recognized it in Hui Neng's "Original Face," in the term "Buddha Nature": it was that specific humanness that would haunt me and result in my "Buddhist interpretation of Christianity" that Narada Thera joked about. This was the transpersonal, transhistorical Christ who would stay with us until the end of the world—or at least for the duration of humankind.

the Cosmic Fish 1986   H.

In a homogenized Catholic town like ours it was unavoidable to overhear that the oldest symbol of Christ was the Fish, "from the times of the catacombs. . ."

I must also have caught something about the Church being the "Mystical Body of Christ." That fired my imagination, which fused both images into a single one, that of an immense Fish. Each one of its innumerable luminous scales carried a human face, large faces on its belly, little ones around eyes and nose.

On late evening walks I imagined the Fish taking off from the huddle of old houses around the ancient Church of Our Lady Star of the Sea, saw it sailing through the black night sky across the river Meuse over the hills, to disappear in the direction of Orion which—was it coincidentally?—had the shape of a cross.

I mused a lot about my Cosmic Fish with its countless human face-scales, and came to the conclusion that it could not possibly be confined to whatever church, however Catholic. It either encompassed all human beings—Dutch, Belgian, German, brown, yellow and black, old Emily and Henriette included—or it was a fishy Fish. . .

Moreover, invisible as it might be to the naked eye, and apart from humankind, my Fish offered shelter to all animals on earth, in the sky and in the sea, perhaps even to trees and dandelions: to all of Creation. The Fish, undoubtedly, was at the origin, and simultaneously at the summit of what became my home-made Christology from the wrong side of the tracks, a Christology so far removed from all systematic theology that it must be purely systemic, generic, perhaps even genetically encoded.

The childhood vision of the great Fish never paled, so that when half a century later I read Fa T'Sang, I recognized it disguised in these ancient Chinese Buddhist parables about the total interdependence—to the very point of their "unimpeded mutual penetration"—of all phenomena in the universe.

I have drawn, painted, carved my Cosmic Fish, hewn him out of a ten-foot tree trunk, forged him in steel, until finally I saw this mystical body mirrored in the Dharmadhatu of Buddhism.

In Part One I sketched out the command performance of Fa T'sang in Empress Wu's palace, this extraordinary demonstration of the "deep ecology," born during the T'ang Dynasty which we have persisted in ignoring at our peril.

Manyness in all its infinite diversity is One, and there is no One without the Many.

> *One in One*
> *One in All*
> *All in One*
> *All in All*

My Fish in Chinese garb!

Only recently, its hubris shaken by the awareness of impending doom, science has come to realize that "God's creation" functions as an "organism" of mutually dependent elements or monads, and that our empirical universe is in constant flux. Peoples, empires, Himalayas, and even gods loom up and disappear without trace. . .

The contrast between the created world of the Judeo-Christian West and the Buddhist intuition of interdependent arising no longer seems an insurmountable obstacle.

Zen: The Homeground
⚜ Rediscovered ⚜

I was powerless to resist my mother's constant programming throughout childhood. She had decided once and for all that I was going to be a great physician, like Uncle Alfred or Uncle Maurits, and so the time came that I entered medical school. Being infinitely more interested, however, in comparative religion and medieval sculpture than in cutting up frogs and corpses, I skipped so many classes, gate-crashed so many lectures on Buddhism, Hinduism, Sufism and Art that I flunked a number of exams.

I was not driven by a thirst for either erudition or information, but by an insatiable appetite for Meaning, for solving the riddle of what life might really be about.

When I happened on my first pamphlet about Zen—in 1926 still almost unknown in the West—it impressed me so strongly that I still recall its yellow cover and the name of its author. What delighted me was that Zen did not estrange me, either from the Fish or from the man on the cross. Zen must be another name for that ingredient in the religions that really made them religious. It was as if I had always known Zen, as if I had rediscovered my homeground, as if I had parachuted into an unknown territory where I recognized every hillock, every bush.

To my agnostic parents meanwhile, my obviously un-medical leanings were worrisome. They must have had nightmares in which they saw me shuffling in the Easter procession in a stiff white alb, a candle in my hand.

They brought the distressing problem up when Uncle Bruno, a well-known novelist at the time, dropped in for lunch.

The great man frowned, then gave me a wink and chuckled maliciously, "High time a metaphysician was born in this dull clan of physicians." I didn't quite know what kind of a physician a metaphysician might be. The dictionary did not make me much wiser, defining metaphysics as "a branch of philosophy."

What fascinated me about Zen, however, was precisely that it was not a branch of philosophy at all, but a direct coming to grips with the innermost workings of life within and around oneself. Every one of the great masters proved it: Bodhidharma, who in the sixth century brought Zen from India to China and declared that it could not be transmitted by scriptures, but only from heart to heart; Hui Neng, with his wondrous seventh century koan: "Show me the Original Face you had before even your parents were born," and in the ninth century by Lin-Chi, who confronted his students with his unforgettable koan: "Show me the True Human-without-status, or rank, in your hulk of red flesh!"

A few centuries later, Dōgen, for whom "all beings not only *have*, but *are* the Buddha Nature," even more poignantly, declared this Buddha Nature to be . . . Impermanence! Finally in our time, Daisetz T. Suzuki, was the sage who—almost single-handedly— initiated the West into Zen, and exerted thereby an astonishing influence on the perceptions and thinking of Western homo religiosus.

I began to suspect that those various religious ideas and doctrines that seem to clash in the brain could fuse without fuss in what, for lack of a better word, I'll call the heart. There they neither clash nor cancel one another out, but mutually transilluminate each other.

I began to wonder, and I still wonder, whether all those irreconcilable tenets and beliefs are not merely the polarization of semantic constructs, and perhaps of equivalent, or even identical archetypes, distorted according to the optical illusions that are built into the lenses of each one of the various cultures.

That so many now turn East in search of a spiritual shelter in our wasteland, is neither mere fashion nor fad. We, late twentieth century people, who have ham and eggs for breakfast, sushi for lunch and Madras curry for supper are no longer living in walled-in cultural ghettos, where beliefs are locked in fixed presuppositions and actions that are shared by all. We are not like the ancient Hebrews for whom Yahweh, as the icon of the divine, was part of the tribal cultural system, hence far beyond even a thought of doubt, let alone rejection. If not politically and ethnically, at any rate gastronomically and spiritually the world is fast becoming a single continent. We find our home where the heart feels at ease. Convergences, isomorphisms, parallelisms in religious experience have become inevitable. A new image of the Specifically Human, the Humanum, may be hovering over the maelstrom of contemporary nihilism and cynicism.

I never became a card-carrying Buddhist just as I never became a Catholic, or even a "Christian," though I was baptized one day by a young minister friend not much older than I.

To label oneself "Christian" and thus to erect barriers between oneself and those Buddhists, Jews, Sufis, Hindus whose religious experience enriches one's own, has never tempted me. The Cosmic Fish, the mystical body, the Sangha are either a total inner experience or else an ideological trap, and as such exclusivistic, just another pretext for the demonic collective in-group ego to violate the full human dignity of the Other, to justify despising the Other, even killing the Other.

I can't help being a loner, incurably allergic to joining anything whatsoever, whether political party, church, sect, cult or even Zen center. I must have suspected at a quite tender age that as far as the need for "identity" is concerned, my (and everyone else's) only real, colorfast, identity is simply to be Human, to realize that "Original Face one had before even one's parents were born." I shivered at the very thought of being caught in one of those nets of "identities" that pit groups of humans against one another.

To be Human included being free. What struck me with great force, however, in what I understood of the heritage of all the great religious traditions was that, firstly, not a single one of these commanded, "Thou shalt kill, steal, torture, or commit adultery." Secondly, that however different their conceptualizations of Ultimate Reality, or the Absolute, of the Divine, might be, there

was a striking similarity in their *paradigms of full Humanness*, let
me call it the Humanum.

I felt the Bodhisattva of Mahayana—the Enlightened One who in
his wisdom/compassion foregoes the beatitude of Nirvana until
all beings are saved or awakened—to be totally compatible with
those Judaic "Just" for whom the world is spared and with the
Jivanmukta of Hinduism.

The *Jivanmukta* transcends scriptures and conventions, even
ethical codes, but can not do anything that is not conducive to
the well-being of others. He is free in thought and action, yet
never sets a bad example. He wears no outer mask of holiness,
enjoys life, but never forgets the divine Self, the presence of
Brahman. He has reached highest insight.

Jivanmukta, Bodhisattva, and the Just were the ones who have
attained the fullness of their humanness—call it *Imago Dei* if
you wish.

The man on the cross who died and rose, had manifested millennia ago the supreme paradigm of this fully Human, manifestation of our own potential of specific, "absolute" Humanness.

Mahayana Buddhism sees it as our "primal" or "original," our
Ur-Natur, our Buddha Nature. Hui Neng's "Original Face," is
what the Christian mystic Nicholas of Cusa spoke of as "The
Face of faces discernible in all faces, veiled as in a riddle. . . "

What the gospel of St. John proclaims to be the "Light that
lightens, literally, every human being come into the world" must
be this divine spark, this True Self that lies fathoms deep beyond
Little Me, the empirical ego.

The precondition for even glimpsing this Light is, in all the traditions: insight into the delusional aspects of ego. It is the Origin,
Lodestar and, at the same time, culmination point of the inner
human journey. It is That Which Matters, under whatever name,
whether in East or in West. It is that which transcends the animal
in us: it is our human specificity! By all means let it be called
"incarnate" in the crucified one who rose: The Unkillable Human.

The symbols, signs, and signalings of the Catholic culture had indeed provided me with the core around which first hints of Meaning could crystallize, connections with the Transcendent/Immanent could be established, and hence an openness to seeing human life and the world in their sacred dimension of existence, of Being.

It never occurred to me, however, that one had to "believe" something or other. One simply had to *see*! The symbols were there! They hardly needed explanation or anyone's commentary. They were transparent! Through them the Invisible became perceptible. All by themselves they changed one's vision of the world, transilluminated it. Any "explanations" could only falsify this direct, "poetic," perception.

I was an inveterate walker, head over heels in love with every spot of my walkable stretch of homeground. A test of such love is to be sad and angry at every interference with it, to resent every new house going up, to be indignant about a new road being built, in mourning for an orchard being cleared. This earth of my childhood was drenched by almost two thousand years of a religious culture that stretched across the national borders, and the linguistic borders where Dutch, Flemish, Walloon and German meet and mingle.

Just as every child is an artist until the artist-within is beaten out of him by the conditionings of family, school, church, so is every child open to the Sacred.

If its hesitant explorations and questionings are thwarted, ridiculed, or answered off-hand by parents—or cut short, by indoctrination pretending to be religious "education"—the child is mutilated in its humanness and is well on its way to become either true believer, fanatic, conformist, cynic, nihilist or any combination of these.

Both the esthetic and the religious impulse, the artist-within and the guru-within, are easily led astray. The delicate tendrils of our humanness are, in their early probings, all too liable to injury.

Pilgrim, Ypres, Belgium

⚘ *A Heart Full of Awe* ⚘

What it is that dwelleth here
I know not
Yet my heart is full of awe
and the tears trickle down.
AN 11TH CENTURY JAPANESE POEM

I must have been eleven or twelve when on one of my hikes just across the Belgian border I strayed into a High Mass, my first. Much later I often took part in the Eucharist, however strictly limited it was to certified Catholics, and even for those on specific conditions. But these were Eucharistic celebrations in small gatherings of marginal, or perhaps they were radical, Catholics with whom I seemed to have a language in common, even if we spoke it with different theological accents. They were as unafraid that the participation by this outsider was dangerously sacrilegious, as I was in realizing that whosoever intended to mock the rite, could only mock and desecrate himself.

I stayed at a safe distance, for I did not belong to the tribe, and the interloper was afraid of being either forcefully removed or, much more alarming, being sucked in and trained to jump through the hoops. I knew the text of the Mass vaguely by heart, from the Requiem Masses by my fellow unbelievers Verdi and Fauré, staples in the repertoire of the local symphony orchestra and choir. It was then still the Latin Mass, so that one had only a cloudy idea of the words, which was all to the good, for it stimulated the imagination and let the transcendent remain transcendent indeed. For the child who had been watching a war from the grandstand, however, the *Dies Irae,* "The Day of Wrath," was not too hard to imagine, nor the *Miserere,* nor the desperate cry for compassion of the *Kyrie.*

To me, hidden intruder, when the little silver bell rang for the consecration and the people knelt down, the awesome took place. Bread and wine indeed changed into That! Here and now they partook of That, becoming one with That! I never thought of it as something magical, had never heard of the controversies of transubstantiation versus transignification, and if I had, I couldn't have cared less. For I knew Heinrich Heine's love poem that was one of Mother's favorites. *Du bist wie eine Blume!* (You are like a flower!) That made it all crystal clear, for it applied precisely to Anneke, the blonde girl next door, whose eyes did not just look like, but were, literally, pale blue forget-me-nots. Anneke's eyes did not need petals to prove the point, did they?

During much of the year pious mothers and their broods were most scrupulous about this "Sunday duty," as were strait-laced burghers in bowler hats and taffeta Sunday finery. But on Easter the families trudged intact to the Communion rail, because fulfilling their "Easter duty" was the minimum requirement for escaping hell-fire in the end. Afterwards in overcrowded cafes around the city square, Heinekens washed down all traces of that which had been so devoutly received on the tongue a few minutes before.

There was a lot of grumbling among my schoolmates about having to fulfill their boring "Sunday duty," but I was envious. What for them was a duty, was for me a forbidden fruit: the solemn affirmation and celebration of the Cosmic Fish.

I tried to question my friend Ernest tactfully, "What do you really feel when you go to Communion?" He looked at me in astonishment. "Feel?" he puzzled, "what do you mean, feel?" So I dropped the subject. Maybe they felt nothing at all. Maybe they just dutifully swallowed Jesus as their Sunday breakfast, waiting impatiently for the pot roast and french fries at noon.

Through the years I also participated in Buddhist, Jewish, and Shinto celebrations and never felt alien or out of place. It was always the deepest in human beings, the Sacred, that manifested itself. The handclaps that called down the god in Shinto, the sign of the cross over the chest, the consecration, the chanting of sutras, the sound of the rams horn on Yom Kippur were not equal but equivalent in solemnity and poignancy.

Still, I came to see and feel the Eucharist to be a rite of universal all-embracing, trans-religious significance, an intercommunication

and intercommunion beyond all doctrinal demarcation lines. It
was at once the consecration and celebration of the fruits of the
earth as ennobled by human labor, and the declaration of the de
facto solidarity of being human. This solidarity, this factual, limitless interdependence was celebrated, not in some wishy-washy
eschatological future, but experienced and affirmed here and now,
in one's visceral identity with Lin-Chi's "True Human-without-
status or rank in this mass of red protoplasm." Who else but the
man on the cross? For this is a universal rite, not just Catholic but
catholic, generic.

Absolute subjectivity and absolute interdependence coincided in
this great rite of the True Man who said, "Do this in remem-
brance of me." It has been repeated a trillion times since he pronounced it, this Human who had radically emptied himself of all
the narcissism of ego, and who pleads, "Remember me! Keep Me
alive as the Human Presence among you in the midst of your
nihilistic vacuum, your inhuman chaos!"

Presence of the Timeless, the absolute Human presence before
Abraham was, Presence that makes the blind see, that awakens
the dead.

"Face of faces," suddenly recognized in the face of the fellow
traveler on the Way at some Emmaus or other, Light illuminating
the gloom of the endarkened mind, from inside out.

The True Self shared as "my body."

Where He speaks of "me" or "my," he speaks of a me-without-I,
for ego has been discounted. There is no Bread that by some
physio-chemical sleight of hand turns into Christ, but the Christ
becomes the Bread shared. The Bread, "my body," is not the body
of Jesus, as if he were corporately owned stage property, but that
of the risen Christ, William Blake's "divine Humanity," Kafka's *das
Unzerstörbare*, the Unkillable, the indestructible Human, the
Original Face, the True Self, the Christ Spirit, under any alias,
Catholic or not.

The rite does not evoke a man named Jesus, nor his crucifixion
but the one universal, Cosmic Christ, who rises from the death of

ego, *theophany* indeed, of the ultimate Reality imprinted on the ground of every heart, unfathomably deeper than the level of ego. To cling to Jesus as a tribal idol not only conceals but denies the risen Universal Christ.

In the Eucharist, the small circle of contemporaries who took part, stood for all of humanity. Its Center was the Truly Human, the Christ. In the circle each one was totally interchangeable, equivalent with any other, yet at the same time totally, uniquely, who he or she really was. For a timeless moment, freed from all ego obsession, they became one with the Center, reflected the Center. They "partook of," they interpenetrated mutually with the Center, with the Absolute Human—the Human Absolute— hence with their own True Self. The rite reaffirmed this contin- ued, timeless, transpersonal presence of the Center, allowed it to rise into consciousness; if only for a single moment, the sleeping Christ within was awakened, the Human Image restored. That moment was no moment, for it was outside of time. In Angelus Silesius' words:

> one step beyond that line called time
> eternity is here. . .

The apocryphal gospel according to Thomas, lets Jesus proclaim, "The kingdom is within you *and* outside you." Both the king- dom within and the kingdom outside us, the earth with all its beings, become manifest in their oneness in this timeless moment in which our existential reality-situation is being enacted and all delusions are made to evaporate. Ecce Homo! See the Human! See who you are! See the Self you keep crucifying!

The Eucharist enacts the central mystery play of every human life. Jesus, the historical figure, becomes transparent as the Risen Christ, transhistorically alive symbolum of who I am—and of failing to be who I am, yet unable to do much about it, for ego cannot "will" to transcend, overcome ego, whatever theologians and psychoanalysts assert.

This, in short, is what the Christic rite transmitted to this non-Christian. It epitomized the reawakening to the unquenchable Light, taproot of all scriptures and homeground of the human adventure, as the full, human imprint which God, or Nature or Evolution, placed in the heart of the pre-human animal, endowing it with the potentiality, hence the assignment, to become Human. This awakening, this metanoia is at once the realization of the potentiality and the fulfillment of the human assignment, the recovery of the Humanum, the Specifically Human, the destination of our pilgrimage from all delusions to the center of the circle of which the Center is everywhere, the circumference nowhere.

Here, as a Buddhist might put it, Samsara and Nirvana, time and timelessness may be seen to be one: all dualities cease. What the various religious languages speak of as: Liberation, Awakening, Salvation, Redemption, Enlightenment, is touched, tasted.

How preposterous therefore that participation in this universal, cosmic rite which celebrates the Oneness of our Manyness, proclaims the sacredness of the earth and its fruits, that unlocks the supernatural grandeur of the natural world, that communicates from core to core, in a visceral communion, is hedged in by legalistic prohibitions. Whatever the theological alibis, it almost succeeds in demeaning it as if it were the top secret ceremonial of some occult sect, some tribal cult.

Merely watching it stealthily, the heart full of awe, became for me sheer "transmission from heart to heart" of that which is Real, central. It might be so for others, if not for all.

One shudders to think of that cozy little church outside of the electrified fence of Auschwitz, where this legalism did not exclude devout SS killers from communion between gassings. Wherever there is too much Jesus talk, the Christic Spirit is apt to be forgotten if not perverted, as any surfeit of God talk is suspect. The Zen master's warning "If you have uttered the name Buddha, go and wash out your mouth!" is not superfluous.

Triune Brains at work N.Y.C.

The Specifically Human
⚶ Confirmed by Modern Science ⚶

Three score and ten years had elapsed since, from behind a pillar, I had attended my first High Mass. Leafing through a scientific magazine in a waiting room I happened on an article about the Triune Brain and the research ever since the fifties of the man who had coined the term.

This man was Paul D. MacLean, M.D., Chief of the Laboratory of Brain Evolution at the National Institutes of Health. MacLean, according to this article, had pointed out, proven, and documented facts about the structure of the human brain and its functioning, which might shed, from a most unexpected angle, some light on what had been the leitmotiv of my life ever since as a child I saw my Cosmic Fish soaring through the interstellar spaces.

I tore out the article in my excitement and read all the papers MacLean had published in the past forty years.

He described our contemporary human brain as consisting of that 'trinity of brains" he calls the Triune Brain. The most archaic component of this trinity is the reptilian brain, which, with all its skills of foraging, fighting, and mating intact, survives in us after its 250 million year history, and is still as active in our skulls as ever.

This reptilian brain is enveloped in the course of evolution by, respectively, the Old Mammalian and the New Mammalian brain. The latter develops into the two hemispheres, which form that remarkable intra-cranial computer which enables us to verbalize, calculate and think logically.

The intra-cranial computer is rigidly logical. It is, however, almost devoid of intuition and feeling, so that we would still be less-than-human were it not for the most recent outcropping of the brain, the pre-frontal cortex.

MacLean was able to locate in this pre-frontal cortex capacities until then unsuspected: the capacity for "insight," namely for introspection into one's own life-process, that awareness of having been born and having to die—which no other animal ever had. It is this awareness that makes it possible to identify with the life process in other living beings. The first stirrings of empathy have a chance to arise! From empathy to compassion is but a step. . .

No crocodile, no cat, has ever had the capacity of a shred of empathy or compassion for its prey.

The Human had appeared from the wings of evolution! A 180 degree mutation had occurred in what from the beginningless beginning had been a dog-eat-dog universe.

From MacLean's findings one is justified to derive the biologically based criteria of what is innately, specifically Human:

When and where the genetically encoded capacities of the prefrontal cortex—empathy, insight, compassion and foresight—take over the controls from the equally encoded but infinitely more archaic reptilian and mammalian patterns of response to stimuli, it is the Humanum, the Specifically Human that manifests itself!

The Human had indeed manifested itself in the chain of evolution untold generations "before Abraham was. . ."

Who could have foreseen or dared to hope that in our time of dehumanization the Human Image would be so convincingly confirmed, so immensely revitalized by contemporary science, hence in that scientific idiom to which our contemporary ears are more attuned than to the theological and metaphysical semantics of two thousand years ago. For it is indeed from neuro-science that these new insights into the Specifically Human are deduced.

What is even more astounding is that these insights into the Specifically Human are so remarkably in accordance with the perennial wisdom embodied in the myths, the ethics, the precepts, of the great religious traditions.

What we routinely call "Human values" are none other than those of empathy, insight, compassion, foresight, so closely connected with the functioning of the pre-frontal cortex.

Arnold Toynbee hailed D.T. Suzuki's initiation of the West into Zen as an event that is potentially comparable in importance to the splitting of the atom. MacLean's discovery of the locus and capabilities for insight, empathy, compassion and foresight as constituting what is specifically Human seems no less momentous.

It confirms in terms of contemporary science St. John's "Light that lightens everyone born human" as being indeed genetically encoded in everyone born human, as the very core of one's Specific Humanness. The criteria of this Humanness are indeed those capacities for insight in our own life process—that awareness of having been born and having to die—which in turn enables us to identify with the life process, the mortality of other beings. Thus the first stirrings of empathy can occur, and that capacity for crawling under the skin of the other, that compassion, which is but a step beyond empathy. The pre-frontal cortex also endows us with the first hunches of causality and foresight.

MacLean makes it clear that the empathic circuits of the prefrontal cortex do not reach maturity until after the upheavals of puberty. He also warns that unless they are nurtured by training at sensitive phases of development, they may never mature at all, and stresses that the "wiring" connecting the three components of the Triune Brain is, alas, precarious. . .

A breakthrough to the Humanum, however, remains always possible, and has been demonstrated repeatedly on death row. The man who committed murder as a teenager may have matured into a human being by the time he, in turn is murdered—legally—years later. Capital punishment itself may well be a regression to proto-human automatisms.

When humans regress to reptilian and/or mammalian behavior, they are all too likely to tumble deeper than that, to a sub-reptilian beastliness and barbarity that boggles the mind. What happens when they are supplied with the tools of deathly high tech, is demonstrated daily on the Evening News.

Ninety percent of all the species that once existed on earth are extinct. If we intend to remain among the surviving ten percent for a while, our Humanness will have to overcome atavistic automatisms of reptilian and mammalian conduct.

⚓ *What Remained on the Filter* ⚓

I started my "detour via the East" when as a medical student I happened on that little book with ZEN printed on its yellow cover in large capitals. It was a few generations before this detour became a standard excursion almost indispensable for the educated, spiritually starved and homeless Westerner.

Taken seriously, the detour is bound to yield new perspectives on the profound verities of our Western spiritual heritage, to resuscitate its treasures from their suspended animation as clichés after centuries of hairsplitting and manipulation for ulterior motives.

Western mythopoeic, poetic, aesthetic metaphors, its works of great, that is—authentic—art, St. Matthew's Passion, Michelangelo's Pieta, Rembrandt's Emmaus, Piero della Francesca's icons, the great Western myths of Burning Bush, of Virgin Birth, of Crucifixion and Resurrection, are of abyssal profundity, and no less self-validating, no less relevant to our own spiritual life as those of the East. The myth of the Buddha's birth, in which newly born from his mother's side, Siddharta "took seven steps, pointed one hand to Heaven, the other to Earth and proclaimed: 'I am born to be enlightened for the well-being of the world'" is of marvelous beauty; so is that of the Immaculate Conception for those who can read it.

The great myths resonate in us, illuminate the mysteries of human life that are unattainable to the intellect.

To "explain" a myth, to "demythologize" it, is to pronounce it dead, in order to justify performing a postmortem on it. For one for whom the myth is still alive, not yet filed under "mythology," such an autopsy amounts to wanton vivisection, as heartless as it is sacrilegious. The great myths, East or West, yield their living secrets, their Wisdom only to the heart.

Reading Upanishads, arguing with Sri Krishna Saxena in London pubs, made me aware that had I been born a Hindu, I could have been a perfectly good Hindu without accepting any kind of "belief". What would make me into a good Hindu would be to attain *Jnana*, that direct insight into Reality, that transcendental cognition which is not merely a way to salvation, but salvation itself.

Hindus distinguish sensitively between "belief" and "faith." Hinduism is so old that it knows how beliefs are time—and culture—specific expressions, mere formulations of faith, constantly changing through history, as they change at the different stages of a single person's journey from birth to death.

For "faith" Hinduism has two different expressions, one of which is *astikya buddhi*, which is a positive attitude, an openness to spiritual tradition, but without any authoritarian specifications of what this attitude might imply. The other expression for faith is *sraddha*, the commitment to it, which I would now recognize as being what had moved me in my childhood response to sacred symbols. Both combined initiated me into what for lack of a less contaminated word I refer to as "faith."

At the same time I seemed to resist conditioning by whomsoever, to reject parroting and could never persuade myself to confuse the commitment to something ineffably quintessential with the allegiance to some institution. For *sraddha* is the existential commitment to what one finds to be true, to be real, whether this recognition is caused by being gripped by the poignant profundity of a myth, a symbol, or a work of art. The opposite of *sraddha* is not disbelief. It is indifference, ego-diffusion, scattered concerns.

Awed and moved by St. John's Prologue and later by Upanishads, Heart Sutra, Fa T'Sang's Hua yen, by Hui Neng, Rinzai, and Meister Eckhart, I found these not to contradict one another but to transilluminate each other: all speak of the Inexpressible That Matters.

There were no jarring dissonants in the essence of being Human they all revealed, each in its own way. They affirmed what I vaguely knew to be hidden somewhere in myself, however far removed I might still be from touching it.

In my readings the intellect did not function as a repository for spiritual or esoteric collectibles but as a filter or sieve. What remained on the filter was in harmony with Reality/Truth as I had experienced it. What could not be integrated was, provisionally, discarded.

I seemed to have as little in common with the automated true believer who swallows his scriptures whole, the way a sea gull swallows a crab, as with the spiritual tourist who flits from guru to roshi to lama. I came to see ever more clearly that God and all ideas "about God" were utterly different matters, and that if God intervened in history, as Judeo-Christianity maintains, our history could only have resulted, not by fiat from on high, but through the life, the faith of quite concrete human beings. St. Teresa of Avila saw that: "God has no hands or feet or voice except ours and through these He works." History, however, seems to prove how He is routinely sabotaged.

All discussions about God's existence or nonexistence, not to speak of "God's plan" would be meaningless for a Buddhist, whose "faith" simply consists in an absolute trust in an ultimate Reality/Truth, mirrored in the ultimate/truth at the ground of his own being. His faith consists in this trust in the ultimate meaningfulness of existence, and in this innate potentiality to realize it, in the double sense of becoming fully conscious of it, and of putting it into practice.

All I had ever read about Buddhism being devoid of the Transcendent proved to be theotechnical balderdash, for Buddhism is not atheistic, it is non-theistic, it is silent about the divine. Neither is it world-denying, nor pessimistic, and even less is it nihilistic. On the contrary: in Mahayana Buddhism, the Buddha's "good news"—and this I understand also to be Christ's—is that there is no escape but inscape, that the Kingdom, the Treasure House is within, and that it is neither caste, gender, race, ritual, or theology that counts, nor one's intellectual feats or mystical triumphs.

What matters is whether one attains to the "Wisdom that is Compassion, the Compassion that is Wisdom," that make one fully Human. What matters is to live one's life rightly or wrongly. Nothing could be further from nihilism!

Faith, in this sense, is not a matter of beliefs but simply of the love of truth and the trust in one's capacity to glimpse, and ultimately to be awakened to the Reality/Truth, the Dharmakaya, that is the nature of the universe and is mirrored in our ground. "Be a lamp unto yourselves," was the Buddha's spiritual testament. The Light this lamp spreads? See John 1:4!

To regard Buddhism as a merely "ethical system" or as a "philosophy" is similarly off the mark. It is most definitely a religion, for it has, through the centuries, transformed human character, generated social cohesion all over Asia. It has inspired untold men and women to live lives of a quality which Christians would have to recognize as being lived in God's presence, lives of wholeness, of holiness. It is slowly penetrating that to "believe in" God (which one, whose God?) is a matter of belief, rather than of faith. Likewise, that there is much in Buddhist insight and Buddhist sanity that is not only compatible with, but actually in urgent need of being integrated in a re-sacralized Western world view.

The crucified man on the cathedral wall, the distant presence at the consecration, those few snatches of words from St. John's gospel, Dhammapada, Heart Sutra, hundreds of Zen mondo, Hui Neng's Platform Sutra, the chanting of Kyrie and Agnus Dei, the vision of the Fish, all had been transmissions of That Which Matters.

Unhampered by doctrinal formulations, they allowed me to glimpse the Specific Humanness of our "Original Face." They did not set off chains of logical reasoning. Doors sprang open as if by the release of powerful springs, shafts of light revealed a vast panorama, the Unseen suddenly became, faintly, seeable.

If faith is indeed the "openness to, the connection with That Which Matters," these were moments of the arising of faith as a constituent of the human being qua human being, awakened, stimulated by the presence, the availability of symbols. In my case the symbols happened to be Catholic ones.

These symbols stimulated that mode of "unthinking-thinking" that is not isolated from feeling. It was a catching of fire, a rising into consciousness at the core of one's being that spilled over, that colored one's acts, one's involvements, one's relationships. What starts, and can only start in the individual heart, must, it seems, however imperfectly, bear a communal fruit. The spiritual life inevitably integrates the personal, the societal, with the Transcendent.

I had learned empirically, quite early in life, that beliefs may not be indispensable ingredients of one's faith, that one may be a confirmed unbeliever, an ethical agnostic like my father, who was the very opposite of a skeptic, cynic, or nihilist. He was simply unable to accept as "belief" what long ago someone else had perceived as truth, but he had faith in his own capacity for experiencing and acting out truth/reality as his birthright.

The beliefs, the verbalizations, the conceptualizations by which people come to terms with their faith are not only culture-bound, they are subject to constant change. To change one's beliefs throughout life is inevitable for anyone who has not turned into stone. To lose such beliefs may not have any dire consequences, but on the contrary, may prove to be a liberation.

For all beliefs, all statements about ultimacy are bound to caricature it: limping conceptualizations, doctrinal propositions, time-bound artifacts, culture-specific attempts to freeze in language what language—itself constantly changing—lacks the tools to express.

the Prelates

To lose one's faith, one's basic trust, however, means to lose a
vital organ of one's Humanness, to lose what makes one literally
see the point of being here at all.

The sickness of our time then, is not the loss of beliefs, neither
the old ones nor those new beliefs with which our ideological
supermarkets are overstocked. It is the loss of faith, the loss of the
capacity to *see* and what the commitment to this seeing implies.

All syncretism is a syncretism of beliefs. There is no syncretism of faith.

In today's common usage, the word to *believe* no longer implies
any commitment, but simply an opinion which others may share
or may not share. To believe in God is an option. You do or you
don't. If you believe that God does *not* exist, that happens to be
your belief.

In the Middle Ages, obviously, belief in God was not optional. It
was a presupposition of the culture, as it still is in Islam. Singing
the Credo was not so much the affirmation of doctrines as it was
a public act of allegiance to these and to one's culture, similar to
joining in singing a tribal or national anthem.

Only since the nineteenth century did belief, in the Catholic
Church, become interpreted as the unconditional intellectual
assent to propositional doctrines. To *believe*, in this sense, became
the criterion of being a believer, "a good Catholic." It stamped
one as being either insider or outsider.

From the time theology began to be obsessed with "correct
belief" as the content of faith, one was required to commit oneself
to doctrinal propositions rather than to ineffable Reality/ Truth, to
God, to Christ. In a world devoted to scientific inquiry, belief in
this sense was destined to become less and less acceptable.

It had been replaced by a new and dominant orthodoxy, that of
Scientism, which also does not countenance heresy. Not that it
burns its heretics, it fires them.

The theologians overestimation of the brain's left hemisphere
may have done more to block, thwart, and subvert contemporary

Never forgotten oak, Noorbeek

spiritual experience than to stimulate it. The mistaken notion that
discursive thinking can make us grasp Being had been an
endemic flaw of Western thought long before Descartes mas-
culinized it so thoroughly, that he may be regarded as the father
of the pseudo-religion of Scientism.

For symbol and myth are not to be analyzed, but to be
responded to. They are fingers pointing toward the sacred, they
are prereflective, preconceptual. It looks as if we might be beginning to respond to them once more, this time post-conceptually.

Could not the present crisis of authority, of communication, of
belief and—much more seriously—of faith, to some extent be due
to the dysfunction of obsolete cerebral theologies cut off from the
unquenchable Light at the human core?

Little Shrine, Waasland

⚜ *Fingers Pointing* ⚜

A few years ago, with a rented car as my studio, I drove around the landscape of my childhood to draw it. Straying less than a mile from the new freeways, I found the cast iron crucifixes and sky-blue madonnas of half a century ago still standing on country crossroads, still pointing silently, almost shyly at some Mystery that transcends the banalities of everyday life. They would outlive those freeways lined with high tension pylons, nuclear smokestacks and the huge, soulless Bauhaus cubes of corporation headquarters and manufacturing plants.

Their symbolism was Catholic, their meaning universal, catholic, timeless. They made me realize what it was I had found lacking in the American landscape, however beautiful, all these years.

I had never been able to pinpoint it, until, close to Maastricht, I saw the little shrine, built in the trunk of a venerable oak. I had never forgotten it after three quarters of a century, and suddenly realized that what I had so sorely missed were these fingers pointing toward the Sacred.

Where "For Sale" signs and billboards cover the landscape, it is knocked soulless, the earth is desecrated. No wonder we speak of it as "dirt!" "Dirt" can be bought, haggled over, covered with mean developments, choked by condos and shopping malls. "Dirt" can be bullied at will, bulldozed, landscaped, eroded, poisoned and debased into toxic landfills, peddled as real estate, that is neither estate nor real.

Climbing that mountain trail near Dharamsala, wondering how on earth I could feel so naturally, so viscerally, at home on this steep Himalayan path, I suddenly became aware of all those little stupas that were peering out of the grass, and the rock with Om Mani Padme Hum carved in Tibetan characters—they were fingers pointing home, fingers pointing toward the Sacred!

In Japan too I had at once this intimate "at home" feeling, for the familiar jam jars full of poppies, daisies and violets stood

Roadside Shrine, Kyoto

around little Shinto shrines everywhere, not only in villages but
even a hundred yards from my hotel near Tokyo station.

In Kyoto I even detected such a shrine glistening in the sun all
the way on top of the new Asahi Shimbun Tower. The Kami, the
divine presence, had been moved there from where I remem-
bered it, on the corner of Sanjo Street. Being in the way of the
new skyscraper going up, it had apologetically, ceremoniously,
no doubt with Shinto handclaps and deep bows been transferred
to this new, this prime location—thirty stories closer to Heaven.

Home is where the heart is not famished, the eye not starved,
the Sacred not banished or desecrated.

The Sacred cannot be caught in formulas. It cannot be analyzed,
not even in terms of ecology, as beauty cannot be caught in the
semantics of esthetics. Fingers pointing toward the Transcendent
need no vocabulary, for they do not preach. Beyond the dialects of
all religions they witness to a religious attitude toward life itself.

✦ A Sequence of Incarnations ✦

At times I feel that the years that have elapsed were more than years, they were a sequence of incarnations compressed into this one lifetime. It is an almost comical, yet sobering entertainment during a sleepless night to let the film roll back. What, if anything, connects all these incarnations lived through this appalling century?

Making up a provisional accounting, I was astounded to discover that I did not choose the content of a single one of these lives that form my life. In retrospect, many of their episodes seem to have happened to someone else, someone long dead, almost forgotten, someone with whom my present "I" seems to have so little in common that I am inclined to think in terms of "he" rather than "I.

It looks as if all that I ever planned or strove for had come to naught. What succeeded just happened.

I had no particular desire for globe-trotting. It was this century that arranged my trotting for me, from Holland to England, to America, to Africa, to Australia and Japan.

I did not choose to paint, draw, carve, or write; I just had to. My parents decided I would be a great doctor. Yet, instead of as even a run of the mill doctor, I end up as an old fellow who still fights his battle with life on pieces of paper, scribbling trees, clouds, human faces, a flock of birds in lines and dots, juggling words into books.

I never chose or planned to teach anesthesia and oral surgery in Pittsburgh! It must have happened to me, as did those exhibitions on Madison Avenue and the Faubourg St. Honoré . . .

Was there a single constant to be found in all these episodes, in this ever-changing pattern of attributes which foolishly I kept objectifying as Me, talking about as "I"?

If there was such a constant, it must be the passionate drive since childhood to solve the riddle of sheer existence, of what being here, and *as a Human being*, might mean.

Each one of these episodes seemed to have been no more than an experiment with life, each experiment a new challenge to answer the question, "What does it all mean, if anything?" Even this "if anything" was never more than a clumsy attempt at being fashionably cynical, for I never had a grain of doubt that one's being here had real, even absolute Meaning, however ephemeral the incarnations, however humiliating, however painful the lessons they taught.

Each one of all these shenanigans contained its object lesson in still having failed to pass the koan, a guffaw at having missed the point again—not this, not this, *neti-neti!*

Each time you missed the solution, you were slapped again, hard, by the Master, by life itself. Each failure made not only you suffer, but those in closest contact with you

Is who we call God, the Master who slaps us?

⚜ *A Love Affair Rekindled* ⚜

My childhood's love affair with the Church, was bound to prove an unhappy one, as such early infatuations are apt to do. Very soon I had detected the disquieting streaks in the beloved that frightened me off. Yet, many years later in 1962, I read Pope John's first speech to the Second Vatican Council, and felt an irrepressible impulse.

I flew to Rome to draw—it is my idiosyncratic response to life—this extraordinary pope and the exceptional event that was the initiative of a man who had kept his unbounded faith in the Human alive in this epoch of murderous and rampant nihilism.

What other pope had ever dared to declare, "God has imprinted on man's heart a Law his conscience enjoins him to obey"? It cannot be repeated too often: on man's heart! Not just on the paper of holy books! This Law could only be the Way, the Truth, the Life, the Tao, the Dharma, the unifying, ordering, regulating, sustaining principle of the universe which demands Human life to be lived humanly—and that is indelibly imprinted on the human heart.

The man I was drawing in St. Peter's, faithful as he was to his Catholic tradition, pointed to, and was by his very nature the prophet of a community of faith, not merely of beliefs, not merely Catholic, but so catholic, so generically religious that it could embrace all of humankind.

Instead of proclaiming new definitions of the exact place of men and women as being either inside or outside of his fold, he and his alter ego Cardinal Augustin Bea prayed with Buddhists, Hindus, Protestants and Jews whom he welcomed with the greeting, "I am Joseph your brother," in an agape, a love feast of human solidarity.

"The Council now beginning, rises in the Church like daybreak. It is now only dawn!" he cried in the midst of the Cuban missile

Approaching St. Peter's

crisis. He was, I had no doubt then, nor have I today, the manifestation of the Spirit in our time. I saw him as a Christic
Bodhisattva, the one who having attained full enlightenment,
refuses to enjoy his beatitude, a private Nirvana, but who
descends into the marketplace bestowing blessings, guiding
those still captive of the delusions of greed, folly and angry
aggression to the Great Liberation.

This Bodhisattva Pope was Wisdom and Compassion incarnate. He even had the Bodhisattva's gentle humor, did not take
himself too seriously. "If I sit on that Chair I am infallible. That is
why I'll never sit on it," he smiled.

After having been drilled for eighty years on the barrack
square, he had overcome all conditioning, all automatisms, and
could be utterly spontaneous. He had walked the Way. "I love
life!" he said. The truth had set him free to embody not an institution but the Cosmic Fish, the Mystical Body.

"Ecco!" I heard him cry from his window with the cancer
gnawing him away, "Ecco! What a sight! My whole family is present, the family of Christ, Father, Mother, and beloved."

He had solved the koan, had become its solution for all to see.
His last encyclical *Pacem in Terris* was a message of supreme
humanness. It was *Pacem in Terris* that I would carve in the
facade of the old mill I made into the trans-religious wayside
shrine I built in Warwick, New York.

"When a man reaches highest perfection," T'sai Ken Ten wrote in the
seventh century, "it is nothing special, it is his normal condition."

It is his innate freedom to attain this normal condition which
Angelo Roncalli, John XXIII manifested.

It was a moment of exaltation, of euphoria, of high hopes reborn,
when his strong clear voice called out to heed the signs of the
times. It was perhaps the first élan of the Spirit in the West since
Emperor Constantine's friendly take-over of Christianity in the
fourth century, a passionately positive affirmation of the
Incarnation, made plausible, believable.

St. Peter's during Vatican II

It accepted the facts of contemporary life. It accepted not only these facts, but celebrated that Life, that Light come into a world of darkness, lies, war and exploitation. It had come to declare that the Kingdom is here and now, that the Other Shore is on this side of the chasm of death, at the opposite pole of that web of violence, greed and cruelty, epitomized as "the Prince of this World."

It looked as if a Christianity of which Gandhi had said was "a splendid idea that ought to be tried," was on the point of really being tried. It seemed as if that prototype of all multinationals, the Roman Church, was on the verge of metanoia—a turnabout at the base—of converting itself to its own gospel. It might turn from defending its all too often indefensible past, from its monopoly as the only true religion, to become truly religious, that is, being present and forward-looking, being open, universal, an authentic healer of the sick heart of the world. It was the moment of John XXIII.

But between the dawn and the sunrise, on June 3, 1963, the genius of the heart had to die.

The old managers in their purple skirts, appalled and frightened by the gusts of fresh air that made the damask drapes capriole madly in the wide-open windows, ran hither and thither to close them, to lure the Dove back into its gilded baroque cage. There was to be no Pentecost, no metanoia.

During the three sessions of the Council that followed Pope John's death and that of his friend Cardinal Bea, architect of Vatican II's enlightened documents on religious freedom and on the Jews, I continued to draw the drama in St. Peter's and its main actors, watching the infighting from close quarters.

There were the "conservatives" fighting to protect their conventions and privileges by defending the honor of God, Christ, Mary. There were the "progressives" blundering psychologically and spiritually in their mistaken efforts to make ancient treasures attractive to TV addicts. They translated sacred mantras into advertising sound bites and replaced with guitar strumming a musical expression that had moved hearts religiously ever since

Pope John XXIII on his bier

Babylonian times. They modernized everything, these precursors of the popemobile, except what mattered, what Pope John XXIII had demonstrated: to trust the imprint on the human heart and to trust it to set us free.

John XXIII had confirmed powerfully what the dying man on the cathedral wall had mutely whispered to the child I was then, that "Christology from the wrong side of the tracks" in which the Christ is the Absolute Human, even the Human Absolute—circumventing problems about his dual nature. My simplistic Christology was not in conflict with as simplistic a Buddhology. Both were in essence anthropologies of the Humanum, the Specifically Human spirit maximally transcending both our still animalistic atavisms, and the ethnic and cultural differentiations of the one human race.

The Risen Christ, the Christ in Glory had been strikingly absent in my hometown, where crucifixes were part of the furniture of living room, doctor's office and butcher shop. The first time I saw a Christ in Glory was in France, on the tympanum of the Basilica of Vezelay and that of the Cathedral of Autun.

The most glorious and most moving Christ in Glory, however, I found in Venice, in a dark, dank hallway of the church of San Giacomo. The corpus was hanging, without a cross, against the rough stone wall in murky half light. I had almost missed it, when suddenly something made me turn around. Was he smiling?

The Christ's face in this austere, twelfth century wood carving was not only serene, it smiled an almost imperceptible Buddha smile. The Christ in Glory of San Giacomo, emptied of all the ballast of the cross, of ego, rising, whispered, "I am the Resurrection and the Life." As Nicholas of Cusa would have said it, "The Word humanized, man deified."

During Pope John's Council, I was still a lonely borderline case in the no-man's land between Christianity and Buddhism. Now, thirty years later, I see ever-growing crowds forming. Interfaith symposia follow one another so breathlessly that soon the IRS may consider them as mere pretexts for tax deductible globe-trotting. Their casts are, of course, professionals: clerics, theotechnicians and self-proclaimed religious "leaders." Professors debate in erudite papers, copiously garnished with footnotes, how and to which extent one can perhaps be—almost—both a Christian and a Buddhist. All too often, of course, they get shipwrecked on the academic cliffs, on hairsplitting differences such as between Christian *agape* and Buddhist *prajna-karuna*, the Great Wisdom-Compassion. This is only natural after a twenty-century-long Western affliction with theological cerebrality. But how oddly off the mark is it in this golden age of the assassins, where one risks being shot dead for stepping on a fellow passenger's toe in a bus, or for merely constituting a "moving target." Might it not be more relevant to contrast *agape/sophia* and *prajna-karuna* taken together, with the neobarbarity that is transforming this paradise earth into a dead-end slum of hell?

Nuns, priests, and ministers find it no more than normal today to practice zazen or hatha yoga instead of novenas and rosaries.

As there can be no doubt of the infinite depths of Christian experience, whence then the need to appropriate those Hindu and Buddhist, often Zen, insights and disciplines? Obviously these have strongly influenced not only the spiritual life, but the psychotherapy, art and poetry of the West. What else could this point at than the entropy of a great spiritual tradition, its betrayal, that repressed insight and orthopraxis by moralism, authoritarianism, legalism and all too exoteric narrowness? Could it not be that Zen and Vedanta act as much needed correctives on Christian routines, a liberation from its compulsive conditioning, from its verbosity, its addiction to word games?

Zen, being neither philosophy nor metaphysical theory, and even less a belief system, immunizes one against all "systems" and "beliefs." It is as radically realistic as it is radically experiential. It

the Sacristy, Rome

puts erudition in its place, stresses the direct, prereflective knowing at the inner core of one's being, peeling off skin after skin of
ego's illusions and pretenses.

No facile consolation is offered, no sentimentality, no hope,
except the hope of reaching the Light at our core, the Treasure
House within that "contains all we ever need," the Unborn, the
Original Face, the True Self, the Buddha Nature, not as some
"essence" but as our total reality, hidden until the moment one
becomes aware of being aware of it.

Zen's freedom is not a freedom *for* the little ego-self, but the freedom *from* it. It is a freedom that may develop gradually, but is
more often attained by a sudden metanoia, a radical turnabout at
the base. Zen's spirituality is an absolute fearless attention to that
which *is*. Its highest worship is to see into our Original Nature,
and hence to *see* instead of to *look-at* the world around us and to
pontificate, to theorize about it.
   Zen is: to be in direct touch with the innermost workings of
life inside and around one. It is not Zen "ideas," but a Zen mentality that has revolutionized the spiritual life of innumerable
Westerners, even if often they are only dimly conscious of its
influence.

Paradoxically, ironically, a veritable Zen establishment, complete
with elaborate real estate and a budding bureaucracy, has sprung
up all over America, as if Zen were the religion it is not. It may
be an indispensable step.

The differences, the contrasts in doctrine between Christianity
and Buddhism are inevitably greater hurdles to Christians
conditioned as they are by "right beliefs" than to Buddhists,
for whom the emphasis is on qualities and levels of consciousness rather than of doctrine. For Buddhism, the world dis-
closes itself to us in accordance with the actual state of our
consciousness.

Buddhism is free from revealed scriptures, inflexible dogma, a theocratic hierarchy. It does not posit a personal, objectified Supreme Being, who is Wholly Other, a God of history, Creator and Judge. Buddhism on the contrary is silent about a First Cause, hence not burdened by a mythical cosmology in conflict with science. Its cosmos is in a constant process of creation and dissolution, in uninterrupted flux, all phenomena and acts in the universe co-arise interdependently. In Hua Yen this interwovenness, this unimpeded mutual interpenetration is most radically affirmed.

This does not imply that Buddhism denies the Transcendent. It has too long been misunderstood as being pessimistic and even nihilistic. The contrary is true. The Buddhist symbol of Transcendence is the Dharma, the Tao, the Law that governs and sustains the *Dharmadhatu*, the Realm, of the Law that sustains the universe. In Mahayana the Dharma is even hypostatized into the *Dharmakaya*, the Body of the Law, Ultimate Reality, close to Meister Eckert's *Gottheit*.

Nirvana, long misinterpeted by Western scholars as annihilation, points to the boundless expansion by which the water drop can contain the great ocean. Oriental Nothingness, Emptiness, *Sunyata*, the Void, are so radically transcendent that its Nothingness transcends Nihilum, the Void is a plenitude devoid of voidness. As D.T. Suzuki expresses it, it is the "source of infinite possibilities." Sunyata expresses negatively what in the positive mode is verbalized as Nirvana, Sunyata and Tathatā, Suchness. But these are not metaphysical word constructs that can be defined. They are Truth/Reality experientially perceived. Realized, they point to a Transcendent which in theistic terms might be called Divine.

The various schools of Buddhism accept one another as compatible, even as complementary Ways to the goal. All see the separate ego-soul as illusory, as a product of *avidya*, that congenital ignorance, that blindness, that fateful unawareness and tragic perversity which makes ego misinterpret all aspects of existence, and is the cause of all anger, greed, and delusion. Sin, which in Christianity is the transgression against God's will, is for Buddhists the result of this primal ignorance, which is not without analogy to Christian original sin. Both original sin and *avidya* point to the fatal delusion that I am more real than thou. Or much worse, that we are more real than them.

The ego to be overcome is the delusional objectification of, the clinging to this ever-changing, ephemeral, isolated empirical Little Me, as if it were absolute and autonomous. Breaking the narcissistic attachment to this separate, isolated, objectified Little Me, is the realization of the equivalence, the self-identity, of I, thou, and it, in the scheme of things, in the Structure of Reality.

An unfortunate by-product of misunderstood Buddhist life-aims is glib talk about the need to "destroy" ego, as if the empirical ego-self were not the coping tool needed to survive. Ego development is an essential stage in our maturation. Ego cannot be "overcome," seen into, until it has developed. Even then, ego needs not to be "destroyed." It must not be clung to. It must be *seen into*, relativized, if we are to be in contact with our own original, Specifically Human, nature. Ego's still pre-human narcissism must rise into consciousness if it is to break its integuments and expand to embrace the All.

For Judeo-Christianity, Reality/Truth, God, is the Wholly Other, all too often seen exoterically, as being "out there." Buddhists—and in this I am a Buddhist—trust to find Reality/Truth, the Wholly Other, at their very own core, its root source.

In Mahayana, the Buddha Nature is seen as the hidden, invulnerable reality of our specific humanness, as "the guru of all the Buddhas," but, as R.H. Blyth says: "We do not know this until our own Buddha Nature teaches it to us." Does this not apply equally to the Light of St. John's Prologue?

Christians speak of the body as the temple of the Spirit. Buddhists too see the body as the vehicle of salvation. All Buddhism's disciplines are therapeutic devices to overcome the *avidya* of the empirical ego.

The theistic religions may see the realization of the Humanum, the Specifically Human potentiality at the human core as salvation, redemption. Nontheistic Buddhism speaks of it as enlightenment, awakening, liberation. For both this fulfilled Humanness constitutes the Magna Charta of human dignity.

I can only see both Buddhism and Christianity as being essentially True-man-isms. Both are powerful antitoxins against cynicism, against the denial of the Human. However much they differ doctrinally, their differences pale when contrasted with that modern Nihilism that denies the Transcendental dimension, and with it all life-affirming values.

Both Buddhism and Christianity proclaim Reality/Truth, but do so in the terms of the cultural and psychological particularities of their place of origin. Both transilluminate our human condition, our human destiny.

In the history of Christianity, however, in contrast to that of Mahayana Buddhism, the paradigm of the Humanum, of the human inner process fulfilled, remained curiously implicit. Only in the mystics, Meister Eckhart, Angelus Silesius, John of the Cross, Boehme, Blake, does it become explicit.

⚜ *Nihilism Unmasked* ⚜

If faith is a central human constituent, the opposite of faith is not doubt, nor is it disbelief or even unbelief.

The antithesis of faith is unfaith, the incapacity to respond to one's existence, that of others, even that of the universe, as having any Meaning at all.

This unfaith is the characteristic of modern Nihilism, this syndrome in which ultra-sophisticated know-how is coupled with an abysmal *avidya* that has cut itself loose from the human roots.

Modern Nihilism is as insane, as all consistent egocentricity is insane. Only by some fluke can we have survived the insane monsters in whom this absurd egocentricity became paroxysmal, the Hitlers, Stalins, Idi Amins, who infected entire populations with their total Evil. Soviet gulags, Nazi abattoirs for humans, engineered famines, nuclear massacres, torture chambers, are this century's unforgivable crimes against the Spirit, against humanity. They have been rationalized, justified, by the ideological balderdash, the bogus religion that camouflaged their unbounded Will to Power. By the rape of our inner sanctuary, the antifaith of Nihilism undermined, poisoned the very substructure on which any social unit can survive.

Nihilism jeopardizes the very future of existence in the human mode. Ever more monstrous cataclysms are the inevitable consequence. Modern Nihilism is the lethal threat to our lives, that of our children, and that of the biosphere itself.

Nihilism is manifest in the tidal wave of triviality, the "normalcy" of commercial and political fraud and imposture, the shattering decibels, the nauseating commercials of "friendly" banks and corporations. The media's corrupt electronic evangelists, the heartless sex, the uninterrupted continuum of manic mayhem they propagate, the shameless lies of their commercials, drug those higher functions of humanity, its soul.

One wonders whether it is the Bomb or the Tube that poses the gravest threat to survival.

Modern Nihilism is the underlying principle of the omnipotent multinationals that empoison entire populations with chemical and psychological carcinogens. It is the unfaith that has contaminated those doctors, nurses and teachers who demean their work to being "just a job;" those surgeons, therapists, and dentists who diagnose our pocketbooks rather than our ills; those lawyers, plumbers, repairmen, and car mechanics who cheat as a matter of course; workers who sabotage their despised and futile work; students impervious to what they have to cram by rote. The immense spread of crime, violence, unprovoked aggression, collective mayhem reflect the pathology of ruthlessness rampant in finance and politics.

Nihilism wears innumerable masks, political, economic, judicial, techno-logical, artistic, even religious. Unless it is unmasked. We are literally lost. The secular city in the nihilist phase of its entropy has become an infested jungle, more dangerous to cross than the Gobi Desert.

Its idol, the Market, its undemocratic predatory fetish, the Economy, are financial artifacts squarely rooted in the Seven Deadly Sins, the radical marginalization of the Humanum, its eradication.

As Nihilism, the dominant anti-faith of our age, colonized both the Eastern and Western hemispheres, the great spiritual tradi-tions were thrown overboard, the norms of being Human forgot-ten, their Exemplars rejected or sentimentalized, recast into "lollipops for comfort."

The fundamental questions, "Who am I? Who are you? What does it mean to live and die as a human being? What does the Christ stand for? What does the Buddha signify?" are shrugged off, forgotten. The resulting vacuum is filled at once with sound bites, bingo, lullabies, advertising slogans.

The churches hardly offer hope, mired as they are in matters of minor relevancy, still indulging in "business as usual"—in moralizing and casuistry, while orgies of murder destabilize that "global village" McLuhan dreamed up.

Nihilism is the exact opposite of what Albert Schweitzer called "Reverence for Life." It is that which has reverence for nothing but Power and Money. It prepares our extinction, and that of all life on this planet.

Meanwhile Christian and Buddhist professionals, insulated decade after decade in their inter-religious dialogue, seem to be shifting hesitantly from their head-to-head debates to sharing religious experiences .

This is a revolutionary phenomenon that foreshadows the overcoming of the chronic pathology of Western religiosity, its addiction to a dialectics of words, and its neglect of the dialectics of feeling and experience. Our endemic lack of reverence for one another's spiritual life must be caused by the automatic assumption that all those "others" have been indoctrinated differently from oneself, hence wrongly. That there is such a thing as a pre-reflective, experiential, self-authenticating religious experience, as such non-debatable, was overlooked.

Could it be dawning among the professionals of the transcendent that twenty centuries of speculative theologizing and academic shadowboxing by the analytical, legalistic, intellectual hemisphere of the brain may have been a tragicomic error and extremely counterproductive? Might they realize that our intellectualizing left hemisphere may well be the least suitable device to deal with symbol and myth, which are themselves the products of the intuitive, poetically endowed right side of the brain?

As interreligious dialogue becomes more experiential, it might convert itself, after centuries of addiction to word constructs, into a kind of group therapy under the auspices of the Spirit, in which the Christian and the Buddhist world views may reveal themselves as complementary and mutually enriching.

Christians may make Buddhists more aware of the place working towards just social structures has in compassionate Bodhisattvic action. Christians, in turn, may learn from Buddhists to take their word-idolatry less seriously, and to realize that their habitual moralizing, their meddlesomeness posing as "Christian love," are counter-productive in today's world.

A Japanese wondered if this much advertised "Christian love" might be similar to the equally touted Japanese "love of nature," as no country has destroyed its nature more recklessly than Japan, and no religion has been more murderous than Christianity. Christians moreover may be helped by this therapy to forswear those ages of hubris, which made them regard all non-Christian spiritualities as being, at best, "antipasto for the Last Supper."

And in time—if there is any left—Christians, Buddhists, and even Moslems may wake up and accept that in this rapidly changing world it is no longer possible to keep the traditional religious structures simon-purely intact, "that the time of religious institutions is past," as Thomas Merton wrote.

Whether the organized religions in their dotage still have any constructive part to play, depends on whether they can overcome the churlish, aggressive self-glorification that is their hereditary affliction—especially that of the Abrahamic ones. It depends also on their ability to switch from pseudo-problems to the central one: the Meaning of Human destiny, the resacralization of life, the unambiguous stand against all antihuman currents and structures.

Buddhist does not have to become Sufi, nor Christian Hassid, or vice versa. For there is no Buddhist, Christian, Moslem, or Judaic truth. There is truth and untruth. There is no Buddhist or Christian or Judaic action. There is human, and there is the antihuman and subhuman action that prepares for a global Jonestown.

Perhaps only a negative, "apophatic" theology has a future, a capacity to establish contact with those many who have become aware that words are misleading when dealing with what is as totally Immanent as it is totally Transcendent—perhaps even Whitehead's "mutually immanent"—and who conceive of the Wholly Other as not being "out there," but closer than ego, yet unattainable, except in its unattainability.

Still, there might be another option.

Professor Rustum Roy at Pennsylvania State University, a prominent scientist, draws attention in his Hibbert Lectures to a pan-entheist theology which might be intellectually as well as spiritually plausible to our contemporary mentality.

Roy reflects on the pan-entheistic worldview having a highly respectable history ever since the great mystic John Scotus Erigena (ca. 815-875) wrote, "Each creature is a theophany of Nothingness." Erigena was quickly and inevitably accused of pantheism. His pan-entheistic view, however, is the very opposite of pantheistic. Pantheism is *indeed* an "ism," a cerebral construct that declares all things to be God. Pan-entheism on the contrary is neither cerebral construct nor is it an "ism."

The term "pan-entheism" is therefore unfortunate and confusing, for it refers to the direct perception, the realization, the *seeing* of the Sacred Mystery as being manifest in all living phenomena.

Nicholas Berdyaev, John Cobb, Bishop John Robinson—the Anglican author of *Honest to God*—Ivan Illich, and earlier William James, Teilhard de Chardin, Whitehead, and Hartshorne have pointed at the pan-entheist approach and its merits.

Professor Roy suggests that the last chance of the Christian churches might be to "give up baby-talk" and to consider seriously replacing the obsolescent clichés that have proven hopelessly incommunicative with the contemporary psyche, by pan-entheist theology that would not only be compatible with the Western religious tradition, but equally with Eastern religions.

It might indeed even rescue science/technology itself from its nihilistic quagmire!

To convert pan-entheist perception into an "ism," would be to petrify perception, revelation, into another ideology.

This *advaita* parable samples perhaps a pan-entheist mode of perception.

> "How does a person seek union with God?" the seeker asked.
> "The harder you seek," the teacher said, "the more distance you create between God and you."
> "So what does one do about the distance?"
> "It is not there."
> "Does that mean that God and I are one?"
> "Not one. Not two."
> "How is that possible?" the monk asked.
> "The sun and its light, the ocean and the waves, the singer and the song. Not one. Not two."

In the pan-entheist view the Universe itself is the context of awakening, liberation, salvation, for the Spirit animates yet transcends it. The Buddha questioned by a monk about the hopeless cruelty on earth, was silent for a while. Then with his right hand pointing downwards he said, "On this earth I have attained Awakening."

⚜ *Fellow Wayfarers* ⚜

Modish wailings to the contrary, communication is still possible, but it is limited to those of one's contemporaries whose interests, degree of awareness, and especially to those whose attitudes and capacity for experience are rather close to one's own. To meet such a person is always a rare, an exhilarating surprise, as if one suddenly spotted a long-lost friend in the faceless crowds of Times Square, Piccadilly Circus, the Champs-Elysees, or the Ginza.

By the end of the Asian part of my travelogue, the first signs of a seachange were becoming noticeable. Now, wherever I go, I meet fellow wayfarers. They mouth no credo, have no list of ready-made answers; what they share is an intense questioning. They may be Christians, Buddhists, Jews, or shun any such self-labeling. They are not true believers, do not belong to fanatic sects or cults. They do not fit either rightist or leftist labels. There are no external signs by which they can be recognized. Yet they spot one another almost instantly, yet not as "brothers and sisters," for they shudder at such outworn churchy clichés that ignore things like sibling rivalry and aggressiveness.

It is as if they founded a new, invisible, totally unstructured monastic Order without hard-and-fast rules, except perhaps that its members must not flee the world but live in it, aware, awake to it and themselves, however painful.

Some in the Order may still call themselves Christians, but they are actually meta-Christians who, far from presuming that Jesus is their chum "running with them," constantly reflect on the presence and the meaning of the Christ in their own lives. These meta-Christians do not so much "believe in" Christ, as they try to follow him—by following what they perceive as their own deepest, most human insights and impulses. They have overcome Christianity's neurosis of exclusiveness, freed themselves of conditioning with instilled taboos and fears of hell, replaced it with an ethic based on insight and love.

The ones who consider themselves Buddhists, do not seek to impress one with neo-oriental cliches. Religious labels are relativized as doing no more than confirm a socio-religious conditioning.

Attitudes, responsibilities toward self and others take precedence over religious affiliation. They have become suspicious of ideologies, especially the utopistic ones that are the most ruthless. What they do have in common, however, does point to a new "religious" awareness, a *religious attitude to life, to existence as such.* It is as if in the face of the threat to human survival, the preciousness of the sheer fact of being alive as humans among living things, had risen into consciousness and with it a strong concern about a human future—or, should there be no such future—about a death not less than human.

This new religious attitude to existence is hardly starry-eyed about some eschatological "oneness" to be attained one day. Eschaton is NOW, at this eleventh hour when even the sciences are opening themselves to the interdependence of all that lives on earth, to the hard fact of Oneness as diversity, of diversity as Oneness which we keep denying at our mortal peril.

Fa T'Sang, after thirteen centuries, is being updated into the ecological problems of the threshold of the twenty-first century.

A few decades ago, it was "politically correct" to shrug off religiosity and spirituality as obsolete, as "neurotic."

We seemed to be living the endgame, the *Kali Yuga*, of an eon that had its great flowering some twenty-five centuries ago, when in the span of 500 years, Lao Tzu and Chuang Tzu in China, the Buddha in India, and Jesus of Nazareth in the Middle East lived and died their answer to the perennial koan, "Who am I? What does it mean to live the Human life humanly?"

The Image of the Human which they left to their contemporaries and to all the generations that followed remained vital ever since, that is, until the triumph of modern Nihilism.

Until then the religions founded on the mythical record of both the Christ and the Buddha had retained their vitality. Their teachings, their lives were still accessible beacons by which the living could set their course and take their bearings.

Then a dreadful amnesia spread over the globe. "Progress" had become the new Revelation. Science/Technology was its Messiah, omniscient, omnipotent. This Messiah's blessings covered the "global village."

After the Second World War these blessings began clearly to show themselves as less glorious than advertised. Exemplary triumphs of technological progress like Hiroshima/Nagasaki, their apotheosis, were somewhat embarrassing. After Vietnam and all the catastrophes that followed, the glowing faith in "Progress" began to show cracks. Button-pushing redemption receded into an eschatological future.

The present flurries of computer addiction, of video and cellular phone devotions have barely affected the destabilization of canonized Science/Technology, the de-sanctification of "Progress."

Meanwhile amidst the electronic din, ideas of Redemption, Liberation, Awakening are assuming a new urgency and a renewed meaning.

It is as if we were becoming aware that "liberation" might mean: being liberated from "Progress's" most destructive obsessions, being "redeemed" from Science/Technology's most absurd follies and suicidal perversions, "awakened" to the abominations of the marketing fetish, "Economy," for which all humans, all animals, all plants, all of the biosphere, are pressed into the service of Profit, of The Market, of Mammon.

Indeed Awakening, Liberation, Redemption might be the waking-up from the nihilistic nightmare of anti-values that brought us to the brink.

It is becoming ever clearer that the terrors of war, hunger, despoliation are, obviously, neither economic, nor technological problems for which there are economic or technological solutions! They are primarily the spiritual problems of life versus death.

It is almost miraculous, how in the depths of ice-cold techno-logical and commercial evil, of anti-values force-fed by the force fed media that violate and negate the inwardness of human beings, once more the primal and eternal riddles that stamp us as human are being recognized as being central, crucial. Nihilism had forgotten all about them, even forgot that it forgot.

Could we, in extremis, be recovering an awareness of the reali-ties of the human condition as-it-is, retrieving some of that won-der and awe that are at the wellspring of all true spirituality, of all viable religion? Could we be ready to be mobilized by this awe?

The thirteenth century abbot, Joachim of Floris, prophesied a time ahead which would witness the dissolution of institutional Christianity, and the dawning of an era in which the Holy Spirit would speak to the human heart directly.

Dream for a moment that Joachim's prophecy is on the point of being fulfilled now, as the poisons are nearing their saturation point, and that the Dove is rising, radiant white, from the toxic fumes. . .

A new spirituality would be on the verge of being born, a seeing of Reality as the Mystery of Being, of being here at all! An awak-ening, neither Christian nor Buddhist, totally Christic, totally Buddhic!

It would be this new-born openness to the Real that would artic-ulate itself in either Buddhist, Christian, Jewish, Moslem, or any other terminology. It would be the recovery from centuries of blindness to see the wondrous fact of being here, of being here in the brevity of our human span, in its unsayable preciousness.

It would be the sea change from neurosis and psychosis to sheer Sanity, from suspended animation to Life.

The convergences, equivalences and isomorphisms between Judeo-Christian spiritualities and the limitless treasures of wisdom and faith of the Indian and Far Eastern heritage are becoming ever more palpable. They must not be squandered on word games, either of the playful New Age or of the academic interfaith variety. At our point of mortal crisis, they must be made to serve as the building blocks for a world-wide "Alliance Against Barbarism" under whatever name. They must lead to a trans-religious, trans-ethnic, trans-national, trans-cultural Humanism that, while fully conscious of the Evil humans are capable of, is steadfast in its faith in the Humanum, encoded in us, the Unkillable Human.

In this one lifetime I have had the extraordinary windfall of having been face to face with at least five of those pioneers who are the embodiments of this new Humanism: a Protestant doctor, Albert Schweitzer; a Catholic pope, John XXIII; and Buddhists such as the great Daisetz Suzuki and the Dalai Lama.

Among scientists I honor above all Paul D. MacLean, M.D. for laying bare incontrovertible biological criteria of Specific Humanness, and my friend professor Rustum Roy, who apart from his prominence in Materials Research, inaugurated the discipline of Science, Technology and Society, and is a theologian of note.

They are powerful signs of hope in the Humanum, in this new Dark Age, defenders of the sacredness of the human person, regardless of sex, race, ethnicity, for which a Gandhi, a Martin Luther King, Jr., an Archbishop Romero, great prophets of human solidarity, gave their lives.

One of the great scientists of our time, Werner Heisenberg, exclaimed at the end of his life: "Science is no longer so important; it is Man who is important."

Indeed there is no choice:

"To be Human—OR NOT TO BE"
is now the Question!
  We must decide to either live, individually and societally, a life that is sanely human or flounder into terminal barbarism.

✠ *Coda* ✠

It is one of those little risks one takes when putting oneself on the line. I confess that both my childhood's dying man on the cathedral wall and his cross accompanied me throughout a life that spans almost the total length of our century.

Nothing in Zen—which I have practiced in my heterodox way for almost fifty years—contradicted what I had gleaned from those early encounters with the crucified one. On the contrary, it shed an even sharper light on Him as being both the prototype and the epitome of what Zen speaks of as the Buddha Nature, as the Suchness of our being Human, of what it really implies to be born human on this polluted, desecrated earth.

And his Cross?

Ah, what else could its vertical stand for than being rooted in earth and anchored in heavens, the cosmos? And what other meaning could the horizontal component have, than out-stretched arms embracing all of earth, all that lives on it, from it?

While writing this I wonder whether my exegesis of the Cross does not give me away as all too primitive.

Trying to find some material on the symbolism of the Cross, to my amazement I meet with similar visions of it by some other primitives, such as Justin the Martyr, Clement of Alexandria, and Hugh of St. Victor.

They speak about the "outstretched hands of the Logos. . ." They say things like, "Behold, that which thou art I have shown thee. . ." or "As in a glass behold the secrets of thy own nature. . ." They call the Cross "Tree of Life" or "the axis mundi" that binds the world together instead of tearing it apart, as do the demonic Powers. . ." In the apocryphal St. John, the Cross becomes "a mirror I am to thee who discerns me. . ."

There is no denying the Cross having been polluted, bloodied, caked with rotting human flesh, defiled, perverted like no other object on earth to incite hatred and murder, "to tear the world apart," to bless massacres, crusades, autos-de-fé, pogroms.

But then, has not Earth itself been polluted, and its oceans, its rivers and every breath of air we breathe?

And yet wherever I may stand on this abused planet, I know I am on sacred ground, where—if mute for a moment—the music of the spheres may become audible above the din of our chaos, as the eucharistic, cosmic hymnody that pervades every cell, as it does every cell of Creation.

"What it is that dwelleth here I know not. . ."

That which "dwelleth here" made the child make the sign of the cross surreptitiously under his jacket. It was neither "catholic" nor "Christian," this gesture. It had become the Sign of the innate Human, of the Unkillable Human. It had become wordless prayer beamed at the Unnameable at moments of overpowering joy, of a fear or a sadness so intense that the heart needed a boost if it was to continue beating.

The Sign exorcised despair, neutralized Evil, compressed into a time-atom, a *ksana*, a *nen*, a bottomless meditation. The sign became a wordless mantra as *"Gate, gate, paragate, parasamgate"*—gone, gone, gone over to the other shore—is the great verbal Mahayana mantra. An equal power in both pulls one back at once to the human core.

And so, at every crossroad, my own and those of our time, when baffled, unsure whether to venture straight ahead or to turn right or left—life does not permit U-turns—like the child of three quarters of a century ago, I still find no answer other than the wordless mantra of the Absolute Human, the Unkillable.

MAY ALL BEINGS BE FULFILLED

The Unkillable Human

by Frederick Franck

In Hiroshima, burned into a concrete wall I saw the shadow of a fellow human, evaporated the moment the bomb struck. Returning home, haunted by this image, I took this steel plate and with a blowtorch cut out the contour of this mutilated victim. When the contour was complete, the human shape fell out. Then I placed both components some 20 feet apart so that through the hollow negative, surrounded by flames of steel, the Unkillable Human could be seen rising like a phoenix from its ashes.

This vision had to take form—straightforward, unadorned—in steel. For neither wood nor stone are the stuff of our age, and it is steel that threatens our survival. I made this sculpture originally for Pacem in Terris, and subsequently have received requests for replicas. It stands now also on the grounds of the Cathedral of St. John the Divine in New York, at Nanzan University (Nagoya, Japan), at Pennsylvania State University, Bucknell University, on the banks of the Susquehanna River in the Harrisburg (Pennsylvania) Peace Park, commissioned by Physicians for Social Responsibility, in the City of Hengelo, Holland, the Cultural Center of Hasselt, Belgium, Buenos Aires Fondacion Elpis, and was just taken to Sarajevo by Anabel Farnell-Watson and Gillian Kean of The Dandelion Trust. In each of these locations it is flanked by the above text.

Glossary

AGAPE:

Divine, impartial love.

AGNUS DEI:

Lamb of God. A liturgical prayer said or sung to Christ as Saviour.

AHRAT or ARHANT:

The perfected man, sage, saint at the highest stage of development, fully and finally emancipated, enlightened.

ATMAN:

The life monad, the Self deep within the empirical ego. It is *not* "personality"; on the contrary, its perception and awareness require the overcoming of the "empirical" or "psychological ego," that which Theravada Buddhism refers to as the "no-self."

ANATTA:

The proposition that nothing in reality corresponds to such words as "I," "mine," that nothing in our empirical self is to be regarded as the true Self.

AVIDYA:

Ignorance, nescience, primal blindness to Reality. The individual counterpart of the cosmic Maya. According to others, there is no difference between Maya and Avidya.

ADVAITA VEDANTA:

A philosophical current in Hinduism which maintains the non-duality, the "not-two-ness" of the central quality of Reality, transcending the irreality of separate being(s) and the dualities of intellectual discrimination.

BODHISATTVA:

a) A Buddha-to-be.

b) The perfected man of Mahayana Buddhism, the all-compassionate one who has reached full emancipation, awakening, has overcome all egoity, yet remains in the world, committed to bring all beings to salvation: In his wisdom he sees no "persons," yet in his compassion he is resolved to save them.

BUDDHA: The awakened one, Enlightened One, He who has gained total release from bondage to avidya. When speaking of The Buddha one usually refers to the historical Gautama Shakytamuni who lived in the Fifth Century he was only the latest in a chain of Buddhas and will be succeeded by the Buddha to come, Maitreya.

DIES IRAE: A medieval Latin hymn on the Day of Judgement sung in requiem masses.

DONA NOBIS PACEM: Give us peace.

IMAGO DEI: God's image.

ECCE HOMO: See the Man, see the human in me.

KARMA: Action, as well as the fruit of action.

KARUNA: See Prajna-Karuna.

KENOSIS: The self-emptying (of Christ).

KYRIE: Lord have mercy upon us.

MAHAKARUNA or MAHAPRAJNA   The Great Wisdom, the Great Compassion.

MAHAYANA: The Great Vehicle, the liberalized reform of Theravata or Hinayana, which between 100 B.C. and 200 A.D. produced a profusion of scriptures (sutras). Although its formulation may deny a separate self, it admits the doctrine that in each person is always present—be it hidden by his false self-image, fruit of intellection—the Buddha-Nature or Suchness. The assertion of this false ego-image cuts man off from full participation in the Oneness of what is negatively referred to as Sunyata, Emptiness, no-Thingness and in positive terms as Suchness: the perception of the world and of self "such as it is."

MAYA: Cosmic illusion—appearance.

OM MANI PADME HUM: The Jewel in the Lotus.

PRAJNA-KARUNA: The Transcendental Wisdom which is inseparable from Transcendental Compassion.

THERAVADA or HINAYANA   The Lesser Vehicle. The orthodox form of Buddhism, as it is still pracitced in Sri Lanka, Thailand, and Burma. It is a Buddhist fundamentalism, which prides itself on never having strayed from the true doctrine as laid down before 483 A.D., set forth in the Pali canon of scriptures. It strictly maintains the doctrine of Anatta.

SATORI: Sudden ultimate insight, Enlightenment, especially in Rinzai Zen.

SUNYATA: The Void, Emptiness, No-Thingness. The Ultimate Reality.

ᴧ *About the Author* ᴧ

Frederick Franck is an extraordinarily versatile polymath.
During his life, which has spanned most of the twentieth century, he has been fortunate to have met and even worked with
some of its spiritual giants.

Born in Maastricht, the Netherlands, in 1909, he studied medicine in his native Holland, graduated in dentistry in Belgium
and acquired a degree from the Royal College of Surgeons in
Edinburgh. He practiced privately in London, but spent his
weekends with a group of Quakers working for the unemployed
miners in Wales. In London, in the late 1930s, he began studying
art seriously.

He came to America in 1939 and received his American degree
from the University of Pittsburgh, where he taught Oral Surgery
and Anesthesiology until 1944, when he went to Australia where
he served as consultant with the then Netherlands Indies
Government until the end of World War II. He returned to the
United States, where he became a citizen in 1945. He practiced in
New York City—but for only two days a week. The rest of the
time he wrote and painted in his studio on Bleecker Street,
which according to legend, had once housed Edgar Allen Poe.
He became successful as a painter and had regular one-man
exhibitions in New York, Paris, and Amsterdam.

From 1958 to 1961 he served as oral surgeon on the medical staff
of the Albert Schweitzer Hospital in Lambaréné, Gabon, where
he founded a dental and oral surgery clinic on behalf of
MEDICO-CARE. His book, *Days with Albert Schweitzer*, was
praised by *The New York Times* as "the best book on Schweitzer
to date" and was translated into ten languages.

In 1963 he was awarded an Honorary Doctorate in Fine Arts by
the University of Pittsburgh.

On reading Pope John XXIII's opening speech to the Second
Vatican Council, Franck felt it would be the spiritual watershed

of the century. He flew to Rome and was the only artist to draw all four sessions from 1962 to 1965. About 80 of these drawings now belong to the St. Louis Priory, another 100 are in the collection of the University of Nijmegen in the Netherlands. Pope John XXIII awarded him a medal of appreciation for these drawings. It arrived as the radio was broadcasting the news of the pope's death.

Franck flew to Rome to draw this "genius of the heart" one last time, on his bier.

In the late 1960s, Franck moved to the countryside to concentrate on his drawing, painting, sculpture, and writing. Today, he and his wife, Claske, live in Warwick, New York, where they have converted the ruins of an eighteenth century watermill into an "oasis of peace and sanity" called Pacem in Terris (Peace on Earth). This transreligious sanctuary, with its gardens and numerous sculptures by Franck, is dedicated to Pope John XXIII, Albert Schweitzer, and the Japanese Buddhist sage Daisetz T. Suzuki. This silent, non-sectarian, sacred space has been made available for Catholic, Protestant, Unitarian, Jewish, Buddhist, and even Shinto services. Its exceptional acoustics make it ideal for chamber music and spiritual drama, which is frequently offered.

Franck's drawings and paintings are part of the permanent collections of a score of museums in America and abroad, including the Museum of Modern Art, the Whitney Museum, the Fogg Museum, the Tokyo National Museum, as well as the Cathedral of St. John the Divine in New York. Many of his sculptures are in public places in the United States and abroad. Most recently, the Albert Schweitzer Institute for the Humanities exhibited his "Drawings of Lambaréné: Albert Schweitzer's Hospital in Action," which will tour the country.

His numerous books, listed in the front of this volume, deal with drawing as a mode of "meditation in action," with his African and Asian experiences, and his consistent, experiential affirmation and personal commitment to the convergences of Eastern and Western spirituality, of which he may be recognized as a forerunner, long before it became an academic specialty.

Ever since he dictated his first book to Claske in 1955, the two have been inseparable in their multi-faceted creative work, including the renowned Zen of Seeing seminars they continue to give here and abroad.

In 1994 he received another Honorary Doctorate, this time from Mount Saint Mary College, Newburgh, New York and was knighted by Queen Beatrix of the Netherlands as Officer of Orange-Nassau.

Each single book, painting, drawing, and sculpture of his has been a finger pointing toward the sacred.

Order Form

You may obtain additional copies of this book from your local book-seller or directly from the publisher. You may photocopy this order form so as not to damage the book in which you find it.

Name_____

Company_____

Address_____

City_____State_____Zip_____

Please send me:

Fingers Pointing Toward the Sacred   Qty___ Price $14.95   Amount_____

Subtotal_____

Shipping: $2.50 per order regardless of the   Shipping $2.50
number of books ordered. Shipping is by USPS book
rate and may take three to four weeks to reach you.   Total_____

Check type of payment
❏ Check or money order (US currency only) enclosed
❏ Visa   ❏ MasterCard

Send orders and catalog
requests to:

Acct #_____-_____-_____-_____
Expiration Date_____

Beacon Point Press
Signature_____   **P.O. Box 460**
Junction City, Oregon 97448

❏ I understand that you attempt to stock all titles by Frederick Franck
    that are in print. Please send me a free catalog of the books by
    Frederick Franck that you offer.

❏ Please send me your free *Spiritual Books Catalog* which features
    unique, often hard-to-find books from over fifty publishers about
    spirituality from the viewpoint of numerous world religious traditions.

BEACON POINT
P R E S S